FROM:

Steve & Samantha

TO:

Hunter and Mary Jane Stewart

Great peace have those who love Jesus. Nothing can make them stumble! Psalm 119:165

The Jesus Psalm p. 215

With great love and honor!

Steve Allen

ALLEN FAMILY MINISTRIES

Allen Family Ministries
Colorado Springs, Colorado, USA
ALLENFAMILYMINISTRIES.ORG

The Psalm 119 Journey
Encounter the Living One through the unfolding of His word. A Journey of Transformation - A 22-Day Devotional.
Copyright © 2022 by Steve Allen.

Unless otherwise indicated, Scripture quotations are taken from the Holy Bible, New International Version "NIV" Copyright © 1973, 1978, 1984, 2011 by Biblica, Inc." Used by permission. All rights reserved worldwide. Scripture quotations marked NKJV are taken from the New King James Version. Copyright© 1982 by Thomas Nelson, Inc. Used by permission. All rights reserved worldwide.

All rights reserved. No part of this book may be reproduced in any form, except for brief quotations in printed reviews, without permission in writing from the publisher. Printed in the United States of America

For information contact:
Steve Allen - steve@allencoaching.com
ALLENCOACHING.COM

Book and cover design by 4TOWER.COM

The Lighthouse has always been significant to me as a symbol of the Word of God and His Holy Spirit. "Your word is a lamp for my feet, a light on my path." (Psalm 119:105 NIV) When we encounter the Word of God, we also encounter the Living One of God - Jesus. He is the light of the world. We were created to be His light in the darkness. May this 22-day devotional lead you into a deeper revelation of His love so that His light will radiate through you.

ISBN: 978-1-7338107-8-4 (softcover)
ISBN: 978-1-7338107-9-1 (e-book)

First Edition: 2022

ALLEN FAMILY MINISTRIES BOOKS
ORDER ON AMAZON

COMING IN 2023

STEVE ALLEN

ENCOUNTER THE LIVING ONE THROUGH THE UNFOLDING OF HIS WORD. A JOURNEY OF TRANSFORMATION.
A 22-DAY DEVOTIONAL.

THE PSALM 119 JOURNEY

HEBREW TREASURE
DR. THOMAS L. BOEHM

WORSHIP WITH THE WORD
JOSEPH MALONEY & MARK WOODWARD
RYAN HALL

TABLE OF CONTENTS

DEDICATION 8

ACKNOWLEDGEMENTS 12

ENDORSEMENTS 15

PREFACE 18

STEVE ALLEN'S VISION STATEMENT 21

HEBREW TREASURE 22

WORSHIP IN THE WORD BIOGRAPHIES 24

INTRODUCTION 28

KEY OF DAVID 22/22 CHALLENGE 34

STEVE ALLEN'S LIFE VERSE 35

DAY 1 | ALEPH – NINE YEARS OLD 36

DAY 2 | BET – THE WELL 44

DAY 3 | GIMEL – JUST BEFORE DAWN 50

DAY 4 | DALETH – UP FROM THE MIRE 56

DAY 5 | HE – THREE YEARS 62

DAY 6 | WAW - CONVICTION 68

DAY 7 | ZAYIN – FIRING SQUAD 76

DAY 8 | HETH - MASADA 82

DAY 9 | TETH – THREE DAYS 90

DAY 10 | YODH – ST. LOUIS COUNTY JAIL 98

DAY 11 | KAPH – TURTLE ISLAND 106

DAY 12 | LAMEDH – PRAYER IS LIFE 116

DAY 13 | MEM – TSUNAMI 122

DAY 14 | NUN – THE HAND OF GOD 130

DAY 15 | SAMEKH – KNOCKING ON HEAVEN'S FLOOR 138

DAY 16 | AYIN – THE OLD CITY 148

DAY 17 | PE – NORTH KOREA 156

DAY 18 | TSADHE – FIVE WORDS 164

DAY 19 | QOPH – THE NIGHTWATCH 172

DAY 20 | RESH – LIFE LESSON 180

DAY 21 | SIN AND SHIN – THE DAYS OF MY YOUTH 186

DAY 22 | TAW – BORDER CROSSING 192

APPENDIX

GOOD NEWS! 200

STORING PSALM 119 IN YOUR HEART 203

PSALM 119 – THE JESUS PSALM 204

MY PSALM 119 JOURNEY TESTIMONIAL - JOSEPH MALONEY 217

MY PSALM 119 JOURNEY TESTIMONIAL – MARK WOODWARD ... 221

TESTIMONY ON MEMORIZING PSALM 119 – PERKY SUN 227

LAND OF THE MORNING CALM– RAND CHESSHIR 228

THE LORD WILL MAKE A WAY – RUSSEL PENNINGTON 229

A SABBATH INVITATION – STEVE ALLEN 230

ALLEN FAMILY MINISTRIES BOOKS 234

ALLEN LEADERSHIP COACHING SPECIAL OFFER 244

DEDICATION

This book is dedicated to my mentor, Clint McDowell.

"Walk with the wise and become wise,
for a companion of fools suffers harm."
Proverbs 13:20 NIV

Clint,

Thank you.

In those two words is a lifetime of stories. I remember Samantha and I meeting you and Jamie after church over three decades ago. Your quick smile and booming laugh stuck in my mind for the next week. Who is this guy? I thought to myself. I've never met someone with such contagious joy; you radiated Jesus. Before we left for the mission field in Bangkok, Thailand, I got to know you better. Over the years, I connected with you over emails, phone calls, and long breakfasts at Cracker Barrel during our furloughs.

In 2007, we moved back to the States, spending a year on sabbatical at Bethel Church. Our phone calls became monthly, and my questions on fathering more frequent, as Samantha and I stewarded the privilege of raising six sons and daughters. To this day, at our Friday evening family dinners, I will ask this question to our family and any guests who grace our table:

"How have you seen God at work this week?"

I got that question from you.

You taught me more about sonship, fathering, and being a godly husband more than any book I ever read. You are the consummate discipler, teaching men who they are in Christ and helping them find their voice.

"Clint, what should I do?"

I asked in desperation when the investment firm that I worked at closed. It was just weeks before Christmas, and you stood with me, encouraging me to keep my eyes on Jesus. "Steve, if money was no object, what would you do?" Without hesitating, I responded, "I would be a leadership coach. I've been mentoring and discipling others over the last two decades, and it's the calling that God has given me."

"Well, then do that." Clint responded.

Within the next three months, I flew to Denver, Colorado, and got certified in a weeklong training for Christian coaches. Now, eleven years later, I'm working with clients in six states, grateful that I get to do what I love.

"Clint, I just got the diagnosis from the doctors. It's not good. They said I have ALS. According to the neurologist, there is no treatment or cure, and I have 2-5 years to live."

It was the end of August 2015, and you reassured me that God's promises and destiny for my life were greater than any man's prognosis. Now, almost eight years after the start of my symptoms, I am a living testimony of God's faithfulness to His promises. My faith has grown through your constant life-giving words and prayers.

In closing, you have taught me much about hearing the voice of God, recognizing the prophetic, and walking in wisdom. We live in different states, and though I haven't seen you face-to-face in five years, we talk weekly. I am amazed at the rich gifts that God has given me through your life. I have grown in my identity as a son, husband, and father because of your godly example. You have generously poured into me over the last thirty-two years.

Thank you.

With great love and honor!

Steve

ACKNOWLEDGEMENTS

I began writing The Psalm 119 Journey devotional in January of 2022 and wrote the book in five months. I am appreciative to one of my spiritual sons, Alex Cullen, who generously gave of his time the first half of 2022 to be my hands as a writing assistant in the creation of this project. The Lord has great things in store for you as you follow His destiny for your life. The best is yet ahead!

I am indebted to my good friend, Thomas Boehm, a prince of a man who invested two months this past summer in researching and crafting the Hebrew Treasure in each of these twenty-two devotionals. A Messianic Jew with two Masters and a PhD, he is more than qualified to write these additions. His brilliance is only overshadowed by his heart for God's people. You will be blessed as you dig deeper into the truth and revelation of Psalm 119 through the lens of the original Hebrew.

A special thanks to the three musicians and worship leaders who wrote the music for the twenty-two songs that are in this devotional: Joseph Maloney, Mark Woodward, and Ryan Hall. Thank you for pouring your talent into this project. Many will be impacted for the Kingdom of God through your anointed efforts.

I would like to thank Sheldon Listenberger, Michael Allen, and Southern Allen for their help in administrative duties with this book. So grateful for your hearts of gold.

I am thankful for my writing coach, Samuel Smith, whom I have partnered with for the last three books. His weekly input into my writing has been invaluable. If you are looking for a writing coach, I would highly recommend this man of God to assist you in your creation. He is a gifted individual who can help you take your writing to the next level. Contact him at: samuel.rey.smith91@gmail.com.

I am indebted to The Psalm 119 Tribe, fourteen intercessors who prayed for my writing weekly:

Carol Gooch, Martha Monnett, Jenetta Allen, Laura Allen, Geri Bridston, Reneé Lastra, Shelly Boer, Betsy Headden, Becky Kown, Sue Poremba, Rand Chesshir, Clint McDowell, Will Lee, and Alex Cullen. Thank you for your faithfulness in prayer for this writing. I am grateful for each of you!

Thank you to my best friend, Russ Pennington, who contributed the song, "The Lord Will Make a Way." This song fueled my faith on the mission field in Bangkok, Thailand, many times during the sixteen years that we were there. Love you Russ!

A special thank you to my uncle, Rand Chesshir, who contributed his song, "Land of the Morning Calm," to this project. I am grateful for your gifting and continual encouragement on my life to follow Jesus. Each time I talk to you on the phone, my spirit is lifted!

Thank you to Tarrah Grabler, my proofreader who worked faithfully on The Psalm 119 Journey Devotional, and my last three books. Your work blesses my readers.

Thank you to Mauro Cavassana, my good friend in Nashville, Tennessee, who is an incredible graphic design artist, web designer, and book publisher. Thank you for going the extra mile and publishing our fifth book! For all publishing and graphic design needs, go to his company website: www.4tower.com.

A special thank you to Michael Birkland: script writer, creative, and filmmaker who produced the video trailers for my book. Amazing! Thank you for adding your talent to this project. Proverbs 22:29.

A special thank you to our faith community here in Colorado Springs who inspire us to be more like Jesus: Lou & Therese Engle, Chris & Susan Berglund, Paul & Cheryl Amabile.

Thank you to the eldership team of Contend Global that we have the privilege of serving with: David & Audry Kim, Grahm & Sarah Foster, and Rustin & Laura Carlson.

I am deeply grateful for Gospel Patrons - Charles & Kathy Chesshir of Cross Plains, Texas, who generously funded the writing and music of The Psalm 119 Journey. Thank you so much for believing in me and sowing into our family through missions & ministry for many decades. Ephesians 1:15-16.

A special thanks to my family who has helped me fight the battle with the giant of ALS over the past eight years! My beautiful wife Samantha, and all my children and grandchildren – Michael and Hannah and their daughter Leisel; Kanaan and Nicole and their daughters Shiloh and Noa; Southern, Isaiah, Jezreel, and Tirza. I love you!

Finally, I am eternally grateful for my Savior and King, Jesus Christ, who has changed my life. You sent forth Your Word and saved me, and rescued me from the grave. My life pursuit is to become like You and radiate Your glory.

Maranatha.
Come Lord Jesus.
You are worthy of it all!

Steve Allen

Steve Allen
June 2nd, 2022

ENDORSEMENTS

Would you like every day to be stirred up to be closer to the Lord and challenged to have more of Him inside you? Then I suggest that for the next 22 days you add a few more minutes to your time with the Lord and let Steve take you on his Psalm 119 journey. Accept the challenge. You will be blessed.

Don Finto
Pastor Emeritus of Belmont Church and Founder of Caleb Global
Author of *Your People Shall be My People, God's Promises and the Future of Israel,* and *The Handbook for the End Times*

Want to walk closer with the Holy Spirit? Want greater communion with our Father GOD through the Word of GOD? My esteemed colleague, Steve Allen, has assembled a devotional tool utilizing Psalm 119 as an on-ramp to the highway of a lifestyle of greater intimacy with his best friend, Jesus, who can be your best friend also.

James W. Goll
Founder of GOD Encounters Ministries

Steve Allen's newest work, The Psalm 119 Journey, takes us through numerous "God moments" in Steve's life as we digest Psalm 119. It is full of insights from the Holy Spirit and questions that can help us create a similar story from our own experiences with God. The "Hebrew Treasures" are truly wonderful and add a richness to the Word choices in the original language. Topped off with powerful worship music created just for Steve and this publication, I highly recommend it!

Jay Capra, M.D
Husband, Father, Grandfather, Mentor, and Pediatrician

This journey through Psalm 119 isn't merely a good thing for Steve to teach. It isn't just a good resource he created. No person has lived the reality of Psalm 119 more than my friend and co-laborer, Steve Allen. I encourage you to prepare your heart and mind to drink deeply because I'm confident the journey you're about to take is a deep well that comes from the overflow of a life of great faith. A faith demonstrated amid great trials, a faith forged by "hearing, and hearing through the Word of God."

David McQueen
Lead Pastor
Beltway Park Church

Steve Allen is a man of the Word of God. He has spent a lifetime filling his soul with the treasures of the Word, and so, of course, treasures naturally flow from his writings. He has walked a difficult road with many physical challenges — a road that would dent if not cripple the faith of many of us, yet he remains buoyant and victorious in his outlook and confident in God. Why? I believe it is precisely because of the transforming power of the Word ingested daily, believed daily, confessed daily. This is why a devotional on Psalm 119, the preeminent articulation in Scripture of the vast riches of the Word of God, is such a powerful tool when brought to life under Steve's careful, insightful pen. Embrace this devotional, soak in the psalm, meditate on both with the accompanying worship songs, and watch as you, too, are transformed.

Dean Briggs
Author of *Ekklesia Rising*, *The Jesus Fast*, *Consumed*, and *The Brave Quest*
www.deanbriggs.com

Steve is a runner. He has spent years conquering the trail, building up stamina, and breathing deep. Even though his legs are not currently working, his speed, stride, capacity, and endurance are only increasing. There are those we admire, and then there are those who inspire us to the deepest core of our being. There are those who break the mold, and then there are those who define a new reality. Steve is one of those rare figures who call us to live beyond what holds us back and to rise to the call to overcome. He has proven this in his determined pace through the desert heat and the limited oxygen of the peaks. If you are with him in running the good race, here is a man who is in it for the distance and for the glory of the Lord. Hear him well, and spend time with him in this book. His words, his life testimony, and his secrets of overcoming are truth drawn from the depths. The words of this book are refined and weighty words, tested and proven, and are fuel for the length of the journey.

David Fitzpatrick
Founder & Director of ICCA - Institute for Cross Cultural Affairs!

PREFACE

"We can do this, Russ, only another quarter mile until we reach the top of The Incline," I visualize myself exhorting my best friend early each morning as I decree my vision statement. I see myself and Russ running up The Incline at Manitou Springs on the east side of Pikes Peak. Olympic athletes train there to condition themselves for top performance. The path is a mile straight up the mountain, a series of irregular steps constructed from railroad ties.[1] One of the things I miss most about the use of my legs is running and hiking. I grew up running with my dad in the late '70s, when running was taking off. There's nothing like hitting your stride after a few miles, when it becomes effortless. After eight years of battling ALS, I anticipate the day when I will run again.

In the midst of my suffering, I steward two of the greatest gifts that God has given us in His Kingdom: faith and hope. When the Son of Man returns, will He find faith on the earth?[2] Every morning, I climb my spiritual Incline by decreeing Psalm 119, the longest chapter in the Bible, which I have stored up in my heart. When I first started, it took me forty-five minutes to an hour. Just recently, I decreed it in eight minutes. The Living Word of God fuels my faith, and faith leads me to hope. There are times in my flesh when I want to throw in the towel. I cannot walk or lift my hands. It is in these moments that the Holy Spirit speaks to me and says, You can do this, Steve. Don't quit. I will never leave you nor forsake you. Remember your dreams. Remember the promises. In the past ninety-six months, I have recorded over 110 dreams of my healing that friends and family

---

[1] Watch this video: "Meet the Community of The Manitou Incline in Colorado | Salomon TV." Watch video via QR Code on page 20.
The Incline is built upon the backs of 2768 railroad ties, with over 2000' of elevation gain.
[2] Luke 18:8 NIV

have shared with me. I dare to believe that God is still slaying giants and that the giant of ALS will come down.

I follow in the steps of my elder brother, Jesus, who has shown me the way.[3] The way of the cross is the way of suffering. Many times we as western Christians are shocked and often offended that to follow Jesus is to suffer. In this offense, many walk away from Him, angered by what this "High Calling" entails. I have faced suffering for years now, and I have learned that in my flesh, I am selfish. Suffering refines my heart so that I shift my gaze from being inwardly absorbed to being outwardly aware. Jesus learned obedience from what He suffered[4] and was able to embrace the cross for the joy that was set before Him[5]. On this day, May 17th, 2022, my body is at its weakest point, but my Spirit-man is at his strongest. Every day, my bread is the Living Word of God. Jesus, the Bread of Life, has filled me with a manna that is not temporal, but eternal. The words of James have become mine:

> "Consider it pure joy, my brothers and sisters, whenever you face trials of many kinds, because you know that the testing of your faith produces perseverance. Let perseverance finish its work so that you may be mature and complete, not lacking anything."
>
> James 1:2-4 NIV

Faith and hope have produced a lasting joy in my heart. This joy is not a surface smile that fails to reach my eyes, but a real, genuine joy that permeates my soul, refreshing me throughout the day, filling me with an anticipation of His goodness and love. Life is hard. It will get

---

[3] I Peter 2:21 NIV
[4] Hebrews 2:10 NIV
[5] Hebrews 12:2 NIV

harder before the return of the King[6]. The good news in this reality is that He is Emmanuel, God with us. We get to experience "the fellowship of His sufferings" in the midst of these trials and testings.

Beloved, I invite you to join me on The Psalm 119 Journey as we seek the heart of the Father and the face of His Son. We are going from strength to strength; faith to faith; and glory to glory[7]. The best is yet ahead. This is not hyperbole or spiritual hype, but the truth of God's Kingdom. He is life. He is our next breath. He is the hope of glory. Selah.

Steve Allen
Colorado Springs, Colorado

*Scan the QR code to watch a brief documentary on The Incline!

---

[6] Matthew 16:33 NIV
[7] Psalm 84:7 NIV; Romans 1:17 NASB; II Corinthians 3:18 NASB

Vision Statement
Steve Allen

I am called to be a father who walks in passion, purity, power, and perseverance in the Lord. I seek to know and love Yeshua with all my heart, soul, mind and strength and make Him known. I delight to love, cherish and champion my Proverbs 31 wife Samantha and father sons and daughters who will change the world because they are following in the steps of THE WORLD CHANGER! As an Abraham, I will climb my mountain, overcome giants and receive my full inheritance as a father. I will not die before my time but live and tell what the Lord has done!

The Living Word of God is a sword in my hands, a fire in my heart, and truth upon my tongue. I will pray it. Live it. And proclaim it; Until the Desired of the Nations returns!

I am called to be a watchman on the walls of Israel and in the Spirit, cry out for her salvation day and night, until a mighty river of revival flows through the earth.

As a Leadership Coach, I will help others break through their barriers, overcome their obstacles to take hold of their destinies. I will wholeheartedly seek to make others great as I help empower and propel them in their God-given assignments!

My Mission.............. is to raise up 10,000 sons who become 10,000 God-fearing, God-loving fathers who disciple nations in preparation for the return of the King!

And finally....................... I will lay down my life for the One who has laid down His life for me.

Hebrew Treasure
Thomas Boehm Biography

Dr. Thomas L. Boehm has walked deeply within Jewish, Messianic Jewish, and Gentile Christian communities with their unique corresponding cultural expressions of identity and worship of the God of Israel. Growing up in a traditional Jewish community, Thomas encountered Yeshua (Jesus) at age 26 in a way that convinced him that He is the Messiah, is alive, and is the One for Whom we were—or should have been—waiting.

In addition to master's degrees in psychology (Northwestern University) and divinity (Trinity Evangelical Divinity School), Thomas also earned his doctorate in special education at Vanderbilt University. He currently serves as the Ann Haskins Associate Professor of Special Education at Wheaton College and is the founding director of the Wheaton Center for Faith and Disability.

Thomas enjoys cultivating what he calls, "Relational depth for Kingdom breadth," which involves pressing into deeper relationships of transparency and authenticity to love God and others well for the sake of reflecting the Kingdom of God here on Earth as it is in Heaven. He does this first and foremost with his wife and five children. Together they are committed to building inclusive community whereby people at the margins of society are embraced with God's extravagant, compelling, and transforming love.

To learn more or connect with Dr. Boehm and his various initiatives, go to his personal website, www.tlboehm.com. One such initiative with special relevance to the Hebrew Treasures in this book, is called The Parashah Project and can be found at www.parashahproject.com.

Worship in the Word Musicians Biographies
Mark Woodward & Joseph Maloney

Joseph Maloney

Joseph Maloney is a singer-songwriter, family nurse practitioner, and lover of Jesus. He grew up barefoot on an apple orchard in a hippy town in northern California called Sebastopol. He spent the girth of his twenties living in Nashville, TN pursuing the three M's (Music, Medicine and Missions). He is passionate about putting the Word of God to music, storing it in his heart and raising up a generation of young men to walk in Purity. He desires to expand the Kingdom of God by bringing Healing and Hope to developing nations through medical clinics and Holy Spirit-led house of prayers. He currently resides in Dallas, TX where he serves at UPPERROOM Dallas church. He has a heart for Israel and prays for the peace of Jerusalem regularly.

Mark Woodward

Mark Woodward is a songwriter, composer, producer, and educator. He is the author and composer of three children's musicals: The Animals' Christmas, The Resurrection, and Maria Montessori: The Musical. As a musician, Mark has played keys with a variety of Christian artists including Jeff Deyo, Julie True, Chris McClarney, Chris DuPré, MikesChair, After Edmund, Sarah Reeves, and Darrell Evans. Mark has taught K-12 Music and Drama in the Nashville area for over a decade. Mark possesses a love for God stories, and he desires to inspire the faith and convict the conscience of America. He and his wife Faith reside in Nashville with their six children, two cats and two ducks.

Ryan Hall

Ryan Hall has been leading worship for almost 20 years and has been part of the prayer movement for over 10 years. Formerly the worship director at the Pasadena International House of Prayer (PIHOP) in California, he is continuing to give himself to creating spaces for day and night worship as Executive Director at the Franklin Prayer House in Franklin, Tennessee.

He has written countless songs...some of which have been sung in churches all over the world. However, his passion remains the same. To see intimacy with Jesus increase both at the local church level and through city-wide expressions of daily worship and prayer. Ryan and his wife Karen and their 2 children currently live in Middle Tennessee as missionaries and have a heart for serving the body of Christ both at home and in the nations.

INTRODUCTION

"I believe that Psalm 119 has the power to break the back of pornography in my generation," Joseph Maloney declared. I sat there, stunned, as the Spirit in me resonated with his words. It was the end of a three-day leadership summit that Contend Global, the ministry I serve with, had hosted. Joseph and a good friend of his had stopped by our house to say goodbye before heading back to their homes in Nashville. In the brief twenty minutes that we had together, we both shared our passion for the Word of God and how it had transformed our lives.

"I heard that you have memorized Psalm 119 this past year," exclaimed Joseph. "I am planning to have it memorized by the end of 2021." I laughed in response and said, "Well, it's my second time through. I memorized it seventeen years ago back on the mission field; it took me three years before I finally finished, and then I promptly put it on the shelf and forgot it." In August of 2020, in the midst of COVID, the Holy Spirit spoke to me and said, *It's time to pick Psalm 119 up again.* My youngest daughter, Tirza, and I spent the next five months storing it in our hearts.

Psalm 119 is the longest chapter in the Bible, coming in at a whopping 176 verses. It is a Hebrew acrostic[8] following the twenty-two letters of the Hebrew alphabet. It has been said that in ancient Jewish culture, parents would use Psalm 119 to teach their children the alphabet, which I think was a brilliant way to learn the Word of God. Some scholars postulate that Psalm 19 is the SparkNotes® for Psalm 119. We know that David is the author of Psalm 19, and although scholars are not certain who wrote Psalm 119, I believe the writers are one and the same. There are seven synonyms in Psalm 119 that represent the Word of God:

---

[8] Acrostic: "a composition usually in verse in which sets of letters taken in order form a word or phrase or a regular sequence of letters of the alphabet." https://www.merriam-webster.com/dictionary/acrostic

law, testimonies, precepts, statutes, commandments, rules, and word[9]. Why is there so much repetition and overlap in describing the Word of God? Repetition is a powerful way to emphasize truth. Over the last year and a half, I have quoted Psalm 119 hundreds of times, and it has impacted me for eternity.

The Hebrew word "Torah" means "teaching." Most Orthodox Jews see the Torah as the first five books of The Law. I am personally convinced that the Holy Spirit was also speaking through David in Psalm 119, "teaching" the people of God, through the generations, of the incredible importance of God's Law and Word.

We do not read the Word of God; rather, it reads us. How is this possible? Here is the simple truth: the Word of God is not like any other book ever written through the annals of time. It is living, and it represents a Living God. The writer of Hebrews[10] says this about the Word of God:

> "For the word of God is living and active, sharper than any two-edged sword, piercing to the division of soul and of spirit, of joints and of marrow, and discerning the thoughts and intentions of the heart."
>
> Hebrews 4:12 ESV

Have you ever been in church when the preacher quoted a passage, and you felt like he was speaking directly to you? In real time, you experienced the work of the Spirit convicting you of sin and

---

[9] Terms in Psalm 119 for God's Covenant Revelation. Crossway, 2022, https://www.esv.org/resources/esv-global-study-bible/chart-19-06/. Accessed 11 May 2022.

[10] The author of Hebrews is unknown, but some scholars believe it was possibly Apollos or Barnabas.
"Introduction to Hebrews." Hebrews 1 ESV - - Bible Gateway, Bible Gateway, 2022, https://www.biblegateway.com/passage/?search=hebrews%2B1&version=ESV.

righteousness through the Word of God. This past week, the Holy Spirit highlighted this verse to me:

> "And the words of the Lord are flawless, like silver refined in a furnace of clay, purified seven times."
>
> Psalm 12:6 NIV 1984

In ancient times, the silversmith would use a crucible to heat up ore that contained many different minerals. The refining process took up to seven times to separate the silver from the dross, which was not usable. By the seventh time, the silver had become 99.9% pure. David used this analogy to show the power of the Word of God in purifying our hearts. When we meditate on the Word of God, it purifies us from the worldly dross. I have personally experienced this in my own life over the last few decades. Each day as I have decreed the Word of God over my life, it has given me a hunger and joy for God's presence and His Kingdom. We are inviting you to store Psalm 119 up in your heart this year.

Steve, review the last few verses of Ephesians 2 in connection to Psalm 119. What do you see? the Holy Spirit spoke quietly in my heart early one morning this past week. I had been meditating on the book of Ephesians for eight months, and that morning the following verses were highlighted to me:

> "For through him we both have access in one Spirit to the Father. So then you are no longer strangers and aliens, but you are fellow citizens with the saints and members of the household of God, built on the foundation of the apostles and prophets, Christ Jesus himself being the cornerstone, in whom the whole structure, being joined together, grows into a holy temple in the Lord. In him you also are being built together into a dwelling place for God by the Spirit."
>
> Ephesians 2:18-22 ESV

In the New Covenant, we are a holy temple that the Spirit of the Lord lives within. Psalm 119 reflects the living stones that make up the foundation of that temple. As we meditate and store up the Word of God in our heart (i.e., memorize it) the house is being built in us. Jesus referenced this house in the parable of the wise and foolish builders[11]. Everyone who hears the words of Jesus and puts them into practice is building his or her life upon the Rock, which is Himself.

In this 22-day devotional, I am using the name "Beloved" to speak to you, the reader. We know that John the disciple was the best friend of the Messiah. Jesus had hundreds of followers, but after spending the night in prayer with His Father, chose the twelve that He wanted. Within the twelve, there were the three who were closest to Him, and of the three, John was called "The Beloved."[12] At the cross, all His disciples deserted Him but one. John risked his life to stand with Jesus and comfort and protect Mary, the mother of Jesus, at the crucifixion. I think it is quite significant that John the Beloved addresses us, the readers of his letters, as "The Beloved." John knew his identity, and he wants us to know ours. This term of endearment is an intimate word that reflects a deep relationship. My prayer is that you would hear the voice of Jesus speaking to you through these writings, inviting you into a deeper relationship with Him and a greater revelation of His love for you.

We must acknowledge the fact that the English language limits us in the understanding of the Bible because it is a translation of the original Hebrew. I am grateful for my friend, Thomas Boehm, who took the time to research and write the Hebrew Treasure for each of the twenty-two devotionals in this book. His insight and wisdom help bring greater clarity and revelation to Psalm 119.

I am honored to introduce three musicians and worship leaders who have joined me in The Psalm 119 Project: Joseph Maloney, Mark Woodward,

---

[11] Matthew 7:24-27 NIV
[12] John 19:25-27; 21:20 NIV

and Ryan Hall. These gifted men of God have composed twenty-two songs from the twenty-two stanzas of Psalm 119. At the end of each devotional, you will find a QR code that you can scan with your smartphone and listen to the Word being sung. May these "new songs" of praise fill you with adoration and joy[13]. It is our prayer that these anointed songs would assist and inspire you in storing the Word of God in your heart. In the appendix, Joseph and Mark have shared their personal testimony of how Psalm 119 has impacted them. You will be blessed in reading them!

Thank you for taking the time to read this introduction as you begin The Psalm 119 Journey. This is my prayer for you:

Father God may Your Spirit touch Your "Beloved" as they seek Your face. May they encounter Your transforming love through the words of these twenty-two devotionals. "One thing we ask, and this is what we seek, that we might gaze upon the beauty of the Lord and seek Him in His temple."[14]

In His Name.
Come Lord Jesus!

Steve Allen
May 11, 2022
In the shadow of the Rockies
Secure in the Hands of God
Colorado Springs, Colorado USA
steve@allencoaching.com
www.allencoaching.com

---

[13] Psalm 40:1-5 ESV
[14] Psalm 27:4 NIV 1984

SPECIAL NOTE:

FROM THE SALE OF THIS BOOK, 50% OF THE PROFITS WILL BE SOWN INTO MISSIONS AND THE ADOPTION MOVEMENT.

KEY OF DAVID
22/22 Challenge
Isaiah 22:22

Journey through the 22-chapter devotional in 22 days.

Then spend the next 22 weeks storing Psalm 119 in your heart.

One 8-verse stanza per week.

This is how you obtain the highly sought-after Key of David.

STEVE ALLEN'S LIFE VERSE

I run in the paths of your commands, for you have set my heart free!

Psalm 119:32 NIV 1984

I run in the paths of Jesus, for He has set my heart free!

From the Psalm 119 Jesus Psalm found in the appendix.

Aleph - Worship With The Word - "Steadfast Spirit"
by Joseph Maloney

DAY 1
The Psalm 119 Journey

א

Aleph

1 Blessed are those whose way is blameless,
   who walk in the law of the Lord!

2 Blessed are those who keep his testimonies,
   who seek him with their whole heart,

3 Who also do no wrong,
   but walk in his ways!

4 You have commanded your precepts
   to be kept diligently.

5 Oh that my ways may be steadfast
   in keeping your statutes!

6 Then I shall not be put to shame,
   having my eyes fixed on all your commandments.

7 I will praise you with an upright heart,
   when I learn your righteous rules.

8 I will keep your statutes;
   do not utterly forsake me!

Nine Years Old

Day by day, eat of the Word.
Over a lifetime, you will grow into a mighty oak of God.

My eyes grew wide as I stood beside the old podium that loomed a foot taller than me. It was a Sunday night in the fall of 1975, and I looked out over the members of our small church as they stared back at me.

"Jonah was called as one of the first missionaries to speak to a pagan people, but instead, he ran the other way."

I'm not sure exactly if I said it that way, but I do know that in the mind of a nine-year-old, this was big stuff–sharing from the Word of God with a bunch of adults, some of them in military uniform.

I looked down at the piece of paper that shook slightly in my hands as I nervously began the five-minute sermon that I had been preparing for two weeks. My father had approached me one Sunday afternoon after church and said, "Steve, it's time for you to preach your first sermon." I was terrified.

"I can't do it, Dad!" I stammered.

"Sure you can, Son. All you have to do is talk from your heart."

"Dad, you know I've never spoken in front of any group before. What am I supposed to say?"

"Well, Son, what are you reading in your Bible right now?" my dad replied.

I thought for a moment, and said, "I just read the story of Jonah. Do you want me to just read the story from the Bible?"

"No, Son; just tell the story in your own words and share why it's important to you."

For the next two weeks, I would lay in bed at night, staring at the ceiling and imagining myself paralyzed, standing in front of a packed building and not knowing what to say. When it actually came to the evening that I shared, it went much better than I thought it would, and a seed was planted in my heart that has matured into an oak tree, now almost fifty years later. That seed was the Living Word of God, and His Word has transformed my life.

It really began at Abilene Christian University in 1984 when I began to hide the Word of God in my heart. In the afternoons after class, I would go for a jog and meditate on His Scriptures. Psalm 1 became a companion to me. As I ran, the words of King David were imprinted on my heart: "For his delight is in the law of the Lord, and on His law, he meditates day and night. He is like a tree that is planted by a stream of water, whose leaf does not wither."[15] These daily runs were sacred times, when I communed with the Lord, and He planted His Word in my inner man. I've literally quoted this psalm thousands of times to myself over the last 35 years. I have seen the power of the Living Word directing my footsteps and forming my decisions throughout life. The big decisions of life–what my life vocation was to be, whom I was to marry, and where I was to live, and also the smaller daily decisions–what I chose to spend my time on, the friends I made, and the entertainment I watched. The Word gave me wisdom for my daily choices and illuminated the path I walked on. It kept me from many pitfalls and steered me away from temptation.

---

[15] Psalm 1:2-3 NIV 1984

Beloved, the Word of God takes time to mature in our hearts. Over days, months, and years, it grows our Spirit man until we become glorified sons and daughters of God[16]. A baby does not become an adult overnight; neither does a mighty oak tree spring from its seed in one year. David speaks of the faithfulness of one who is steadfast with the Word of God. If we want to grow in faithfulness, we must grow the Word of God in our hearts.

> "Oh that my ways may be steadfast
> in keeping your statutes!"
>
> Psalm 119:5 ESV

Trust God's character development plan. He is for you and loves you. His heart is to see you grow into the image of His Son. We are destined to look like Jesus. Father God is patient with us as we grow up into Him. In the verse below, we see God's plan and destiny for our lives. As we allow the seed of God's Word to be planted in our hearts, germinate, and grow, we will rise up to become mighty oaks of God. We will display His splendor in our daily walk, family life, and the work of our hands. Be encouraged in the journey, my friend, if you see yourself only as a small sapling. Trust that God the Father is at work and will grow you up into a mighty tree that will reflect His glory.

> "They will be called oaks of righteousness,
> a planting of the Lord for the display of his splendor."
>
> Isaiah 61:3b NIV

---

[16] Hebrews 2:10 NIV

Journal

Ask the Holy Spirit to give you revelation of the treasure that is hidden away in these names for the Word of God. How are they different? What stands out to you?

Word

Laws

Testimonies

Precepts

Statutes

Commands

Rules

Promises

Ways

Prayer

Father God, thank You for the revelation of the Word of God that You are showing me. Thank You that Your Spirit is giving me insight and understanding that I never had before, that is leading me into a deeper relationship with You, and a love for Your Word.

In the Name of Jesus!

Hebrew Treasure
Thomas L. Boehm

א Aleph

Your heart can be joyfully satisfied. *Ashrei* (אַשְׁרֵי) is the first word of this psalm and this Hebrew word begins with the Hebrew letter *aleph* (א) – the 1st letter in the Hebrew alphabet. As an acrostic poem, each of the eight verses in every stanza of Psalm 119, begins with the same Hebrew letter. Furthermore, each stanza corresponds to the order of the letters of the Hebrew alphabet. In other words, *aleph* begins the first word in each of the first eight verses of Psalm 119, the next Hebrew letter, *bet*, begins the first word of each of the eight verses in the second stanza, etc. In this first stanza, *Ashrei* is actually the first word in both verses 1 and 2 and while often translated "blessed," actually describes a deeper experience of being "joyfully satisfied." Think about that. What makes you joyfully satisfied? Just as the entire Psalter opens with two introductory *psalms*, Psalm 119 opens with two introductory *verses* pointing us to this state of richest blessing that God desires for all His children. While *ashrei* sometimes gets translated as "happy," this is a far too superficial description of the inheritance of our full blessing as a beloved child of God. For example, Psalm 1 also opens with the word *ashrei* as a description of the inheritance for the one who "delights in the law of the Lord" (Ps. 1:1). Similarly, Psalm 119 invites us deeper into God's instructions as the pathway deeper into His heart of love. Additionally, in the Sermon on the Mount, each of the eight verses of Matthew 5:3-10, begins with the Greek, *makarios*, or "blessed." Better known by the Latin influenced term *"beatitudes,"* *makarios* is actually a translation of the Hebrew *ashrei*. As God's beloved Son, Jesus extended the Father's covenant love to all with ears to hear, faith to believe, and a will to obey. Go deeper into the Father's heart today. Seek God's voice through His Word – written and living – and the blessings of being *joyfully satisfied* in Him. Soul contentment through abiding communion with Jesus is the only path to true joyful satisfaction!

Bet - Worship with The Word - "The Pure Journey"
by Ryan Hall

DAY 2
The Psalm 119 Journey

א

Bet

9 How can a young man keep his way pure?
  By guarding it according to your word.

10 With my whole heart I seek you;
   let me not wander from your commandments!

11 I have stored up your word in my heart,
   that I might not sin against you.

12 Blessed are you, O Lord;
   teach me your statutes!

13 With my lips I declare
   all the rules of your mouth.

14 In the way of your testimonies I delight
   as much as in all riches.

15 I will meditate on your precepts
   and fix my eyes on your ways.

16 I will delight in your statutes;
   I will not forget your word.

The Well

The Word and the Spirit.
Living Water that will never run dry.

The woman blushed and looked away. She hesitated to answer the question that this man, obviously a prophet, was asking her:

"Where is your husband? Go and get him."

"I have no husband," she replied.

Jesus said to her, "You are right when you say you have no husband. The fact is, you have had five husbands, and the man you now have is not your husband. What you have just said is quite true[17]."

Speaking the truth in love, Jesus gently exposed the duplicity of the Samaritan woman's life. She was alone in the noonday heat, drawing water by herself because she was an outcast as a result of the life she lived. Jesus offered her something that she had never received–living water that would quench the thirst of her soul.

In my youth, I loved reading the Word of God and sought to honor His ways by keeping my heart pure; it was an uphill battle. In the days before the Internet and cell phones, I found myself in the photography section of bookstores looking at images of naked women. I struggled with lust and felt defiled by it. Many nights, I would pray for the Lord to forgive me, but would often end up in the same muddy pit.

---

[17] John 4:17-18 ESV

> "How can a young man keep his way pure?
> By guarding it according to your word."

Psalm 119:9 ESV

How can a young man keep his way pure? The passage above says that the Word of God has the power to cleanse a man's heart and keep him from the shackles of the flesh. I tried for many years as a teenager to overcome this stronghold, but failed on my own. The enemy traffics in the shadows through fear and shame. He seeks to enslave millions under his dominion. Through isolation and intimidation, he drives the sons of men into darkness. In this foreboding silence, he curses and accuses them of flagrant sin.

It was not until I met the Holy Spirit, the Living Water, that I found freedom. Beloved, it is the Word and the Spirit that will empower you to overcome the temptations of the evil one[18]. Jesus offered the woman at the well something that she had never heard of before: Living Water. This water is the presence of the Holy Spirit in our lives.

Many people are trying to live the Christian life through their own strength and willpower. It just doesn't work. It's what I call "Constipated Christianity." You try really hard but don't get very far, and it ends up stinking for you and for everyone around you. The Holy Spirit is a part of the Trinity, guiding us into all truth and giving us counsel and wisdom.[19] He is a deposit guaranteeing our inheritance, and He empowers us to run the race set before us. He only speaks what He hears the Father speaking. He warns us of pitfalls and temptations. Paul encourages us with these words: "Since

---

[18] John 4:23-24 ESV
[19] John 16:13 NIV

we live by the Spirit, let us keep in step with the Spirit."[20]

The Word and the Spirit. When we walk with both of these gifts of God, we are empowered to overcome the enemy. We were not meant to just barely get by in this life, with each day a struggle to keep our head above water. We were meant to be more than conquerors;[21] to wield the Sword of the Spirit, the Word of God; and to run in the power of the Spirit, not growing weary.[22]

Journal

What have you learned about the battle of purity over the course of your lifetime?

Where has the enemy been attacking you?

How can the Word of God be a powerful weapon in your hands to overcome the enemy?

Thirty Day Challenge: Memorize Psalm 119:9-16 in the next seven days and decree it daily for the next thirty!

Prayer

King Jesus, thank You that You are not only Savior, but Lord of my life. I surrender my heart, soul, and mind to you, that You would reign and rule over me. Thank You that it is by Your Spirit and the Word that I overcome the lust of the flesh. Forgive me for times when I have sought comfort and distraction in the things of the world. Thank You

---

[20] Galatians 5:25 NIV 1984
[21] Romans 8:37 NIV
[22] Ephesians 6:17 NIV

that You have given me Your robes of righteousness. In Your purity, I become pure.
In the Name of Jesus!

Hebrew Treasure
Thomas L. Boehm

ב Bet

Baruch (בָּרוּךְ) is the first Hebrew word in Psalm 119:12 and begins with the letter bet/vet (ב). By translating this word as "blessed," however, most English versions blur distinctions between the underlying Hebrew words: baruch and ashrei. As mentioned above, ashrei (vv. 1, 2), means joyfully satisfied and reflects our state of being blessed. Conversely here, baruch, comes from the Hebrew root word meaning "to bless" and points to the act of giving a blessing, rather than receiving a blessing. In other words, the word baruch is one that ascribes worth and imparts blessing. With this word, the writer is blessing God as the One to Whom blessing is due. In fact, the opening phrase in v. 12, "Blessed are you, O Lord" translates the Hebrew, "Baruch Atah ADONAI," which is the way most traditional Hebrew blessings begin. After blessing God, the writer goes on to petition God for help in learning His statutes crying out, "teach me your statutes." Praise before petition. Adoration before asking. As God's beloved, our Heavenly Father desires to pour out His blessings upon you. One of the ways God leads you deeper into receiving His blessing is by drawing your attention off of yourself and more onto God and others and to be one who blesses. This is one reason it is truly better to give than to receive. Go forth today and baruch God and others!

Gimel - Worship with the Word - "Deal Bountifully"
by Mark Woodward

DAY 3
The Psalm 119 Journey

ג

Gimel

17 Deal bountifully with your servant,
   that I may live and keep your word.

18 Open my eyes, that I may behold
   wondrous things out of your law.

19 I am a sojourner on the earth;
   hide not your commandments from me!

20 My soul is consumed with longing
   for your rules at all times.

21 You rebuke the insolent, accursed ones,
   who wander from your commandments.

22 Take away from me scorn and contempt,
   for I have kept your testimonies.

23 Even though princes sit plotting against me,
   your servant will meditate on your statutes.

24 Your testimonies are my delight;
   they are my counselors.

Just Before Dawn
He is speaking, Beloved.
Listen to His voice.

I opened my eyes slowly as the numbers on the ceiling above me swam into focus: 4:30 a.m. For Christmas, I had asked for a new digital clock that would project the time onto the bedroom ceiling so that I did not have to lift my head off the pillow to see it. Seven years into my battle with ALS, my muscles have atrophied and do not allow me to sit up in bed. It was five days into the new year of 2022, and I slept, on average, six hours nightly. This often left several hours of being awake before my wife, Samantha, got up to have her quiet time. I did not want to bother her and interrupt her precious sleep, so I would pray and meditate on the Word. For over a year, I had been quoting Psalm 119 twice a week, on Tuesday and Saturday mornings, to keep it fresh in my heart.

Son, I want you to make Psalm 119 part of your daily bread each morning, the Lord spoke quietly in my heart. I recognized His voice and was immediately gripped by the opportunity to be washed daily in the Living Word. This is going to be amazing! I thought to myself. For the next week and a half, I would wake up around 4:30 a.m., and for 30-40 minutes I would decree Psalm 119 softly, as to not disturb Samantha.

About six months ago, I got some pushback: "Why are you spending so much time on this chapter?" one person asked. "Psalm 119 is all about the law." I knew what he meant. We are now under the New Covenant and live by grace. I smiled and responded, "Jesus Himself said in the Beatitudes that He did not come to abolish the law, but to fulfill it."[23] In the book of John, it says that in the beginning was the

---

[23] Matthew 5:17-20 NIV

Word, and the Word was with God, and the Word was God."[24] One of my favorite verses in the whole Bible is in the same chapter, where it says, "The Word became flesh and dwelt among us."[25] Psalm 119 is a forerunner to John 1:1. The Word of God is living and active; it is not dead words in a dusty history book, but rather the living breath of God.

A week later, before daybreak, the Holy Spirit dropped a thought in my heart - *Go back through Psalm 119, and every time you see a synonym for the Word of God, replace it with the name "Jesus."*[26] I thought to myself, This is brilliant. It gives fresh insight into the longest chapter of the Bible. It was always about Him!

Here is an example of replacing "your commands" with "**Jesus**," using my life verse, Psalm 119:32:[27]

> "I run in the path of your commands,
> for you have set my heart free."

> "I run in the path of **Jesus**,
> for you have set my heart free."

For my birthday this past April, my wife, Samantha, had an artist friend of hers mount this verse above the bay window in our dining room that opens up to the view of Pikes Peak.

Go to the appendix to see Psalm 119 in its entirety with "**Jesus**" in His rightful place. I call it The Jesus Psalm. May it refresh your heart and draw you closer to His Living Word. Beloved, remember that the

---

[24] John 1:1 NIV
[25] John 1:14 NIV
[26] See appendix for The Jesus Psalm 119
[27] NIV 1984

law leads us to grace.[28] It is the foundation that the cross stands upon. He is the Rock of Ages.

Recently, Samantha shared a powerful exhortation with me from Bill Johnson on the Word of God. He was listening to a message on the underground church in China, and the preacher said that those who had memorized the Word of God were able to persevere in the midst of great persecution, but those who had not, fell away. Bill then made this comment:

"The Word still has to become flesh."

Beloved, when we embrace the Word of God into our hearts, memorizing it, taking ownership of it by asking the Holy Spirit to imprint it upon our spirits, then the Word truly will become flesh. Psalm 119 has become imprinted on my heart. After hundreds of times decreeing it, the Word is becoming flesh in me. Selah.

Journal

Read slowly through these eight verses of Psalm 119:17-24. What is the Holy Spirit revealing to you?

Ask Him to open the eyes of your heart so that you would see "wondrous things"[29] in His Word.

How does meditation on His Word keep you from the snares of the enemy?

---

[28] Galatians 3:19-25 NIV
[29] Psalm 119:18 ESV

Prayer

Father God, increase the hunger in my heart for Your Living Bread - Your Word. May Your Scriptures become my daily bread. Just as an athlete hungers for whole foods, fresh vegetables, and ripe fruits, may my spirit hunger for Your life-giving Truth.

In the Name of Jesus!

Hebrew Treasure
Thomas L. Boehm

Gimel ג

As a prayer, this stanza is the antidote for spiritual blindness. The word Gal (גל) means "to uncover or remove" and begins with the Hebrew letter gimel (ג). The word appears twice in this stanza as the root of the first word in verses 18 ("open my eyes") and 22 ("Take away from me scorn and contempt"). The writer is using this word gal to cry out to God for an unveiling of his own eyes (v. 18) and for vindication from the attack of others (v. 22). In verse 18, some translations define "open" as "unveil." The Apostle Paul describes the spiritual opening of eyes by unveiling them in 2 Corinthians 3:12-18. Specifically, he speaks of unveiling eyes through the Holy Spirit's power to take the seed of faith — faith required to turn and fully surrender to the Lord — and to create a person who radiates the glory of God. Similarly in Romans 11, Paul exhorts believers to pray for an unveiling of Jewish eyes to behold their Messiah (although Paul strongly cautions us not to be arrogant towards Jewish people who don't yet know Jesus), and he warns against ignorance of God's ultimate plans for Jewish restoration and the restoration of all things. With unveiled and spiritually open eyes of faith, you can see and savor Jesus to follow Him wholeheartedly – even as He fully sees and loves you (1 Cor. 13:12)! Try using these God-breathed words to cry out daily to Him to remove the veil from your eyes so you can better behold His Beloved Son; He is the ultimate "wondrous thing" (v. 18)!

Daleth - Worship with the Word - "You Answered Me" by Ryan Hall

DAY 4

The Psalm 119 Journey

ג

Daleth

25 My soul clings to the dust;
   give me life according to your word!

26 When I told of my ways, you answered me;
   teach me your statutes!

27 Make me understand the way of your precepts,
   and I will meditate on your wondrous works.

28 My soul melts away for sorrow;
   strengthen me according to your word!

29 Put false ways far from me
   and graciously teach me your law!

30 I have chosen the way of faithfulness;
   I set your rules before me.

31 I cling to your testimonies, O Lord;
   let me not be put to shame!

32 I will run in the way of your commandments
   when you enlarge my heart!

Up From the Mire
Man is but humble dust,
But from this lifeless state, He has given us eternity.

Rain fell steadily as we trekked up the steep path to the Kären village in the mountains of northern Thailand. Water dripped off the top of my hooded poncho, impairing my vision and creating a mist from the heat and humidity. My calves were aching and my toes blistering; we were still several hours away. My rubber sandals were covered in a thick layer of red mud that I knew would leave a permanent stain, a souvenir from our trip.

As I walked, a thought entered my mind:

Was the clay that Father God used to make Adam like this mud?

I continued to slog through the red muck, thinking.

What was it like when Adam breathed his first breath?

What an amazing God He is, and what a humbling beginning to our existence, that He would create life out of the very mire of the earth.

Look at the first verse, Psalm 119:25, in the Daleth stanza:

> "My soul clings to the dust;
> give me life according to your word!"

Go with me to the beginning...

The Creator of the universe stooped down and with both hands, scooped up the rich red dirt of the land of Havilah.[30] A smile crossed His face as a thought came into existence –This will be My finest creation. He spat into the dirt and started to work the mixture into clay. Time stood still as a figure appeared out of the terra cotta. First, a head was formed, then arms, a torso, and then legs. Yahweh worked with incredible speed and efficiency. The Master Artist was creating His magnum opus. Finally, He stood up and looked down at the body.

Now, my Spirit will enter him. The dust will become life. Gently, the Father of Life picked up the man and placed His mouth upon his mouth, slowly breathing the very essence of being into the earthen body. The clay began turning color as flesh covered the man. The body became warm in the Creator's hands. Blood began to flow through a million capillaries. With a gasp, the man opened his mouth and breathed in oxygen for the first time. His eyes slowly opened as he focused on the face of the Ancient of Days. Reflected in His eyes, the man showed great intelligence that was bequeathed to him when the breath of life entered. The Father smiled as He looked down upon His creation. The smile had a life of its own and found itself on the face of the man. The smile burst into life as the man's face beamed, and his eyes danced. "Abba… Abba…" The son of earth spoke the first words of humanity. Mankind had just been birthed into the cosmos.

Beloved, we all came from the dust, and these temporal earthen bodies will return to the dust. Our Creator is Spirit, and He gave us His Spirit to reside in us. The psalmist says in verse 25 that our life comes from His Word. Do you understand how powerful and significant this is? His Word is life. His breath is the Living Word.[31] Our spirits

---

[30] Genesis 2:7-11
[31] "The Spirit gives life; the flesh counts for nothing. The words I have spoken to you—they are full of the Spirit and life." John 6:63 NIV

are eternal and will live throughout eternity. The words that we read and meditate upon in the literary masterpiece of Psalm 119 are life-giving and point to the Life-Giver. Selah.

Journal

Why would Father God create you out of the dust?

What is He showing to you about your identity and purpose through how He created you?

Prayer

Abba, thank You that You have breathed life into me and have filled me with life eternal. Thank You that my whole existence rests upon Your Word.[32] Your Breath is Your Word, and my life is brimming with it. I am completely filled with awe and humble gratitude. I love You, Papa!

In the Name of Jesus!

Hebrew Treasure
Thomas L. Boehm

ד Daleth

If a dear friend invited you to a party, your first question might be, where is it? Secondly, if you wanted to go you would need to decide how to get there. Derech (דֶּרֶךְ) is the Hebrew word meaning "the way, path, or road" and begins with the letter daleth (ד). The treasure here, however, is found not by seeking to answer the "where" or "how"

---

[32] Hebrews 1:3 NIV

questions, but to prioritize savoring the answer to the question of "who." Derech is the root of the opening word in five (vv. 26, 27, 29, 30, 32) of the eight verses in this stanza. "The way" typically refers to a person's manner of living or the path of their life. The psalmist describes telling God the "how" of his living in verse 26 and commits himself to pursuing God's "how" for a faithfully obedient life that is pleasing to Him in the remaining four verses. Thomas, the disciple who needed more explicit revelation to believe (Jn. 20:25), posed the "where" question to Jesus, "Lord, we don't know where you are going, so how can we know the way?" (Jn. 14:5) to which, "Jesus answered, 'I am the way'..." (Jn. 14:6). The Messiah is the way. By fixing our eyes on Him, we are led to each "where" God has for us in life whether those circumstances are pleasant or unpleasant. Furthermore, by fixing our eyes on Jesus we continually learn the "how" of faith-fueled obedience. Beloved, keep your eyes on Jesus, the One who alone knows where and how to lead you deeper into the Father's love.

Hey - Worship with the Word - "God, My Teacher"
by Joseph Maloney

DAY 5

The Psalm 119 Journey

ה

Hey

33 Teach me, O Lord, the way of your statutes;
   and I will keep it to the end.

34 Give me understanding, that I may keep your law
   and observe it with my whole heart.

35 Lead me in the path of your commandments,
   for I delight in it.

36 Incline my heart to your testimonies,
   and not to selfish gain!

37 Turn my eyes from looking at worthless things;
   and give me life in your ways.

38 Confirm to your servant your promise,
   that you may be feared.

39 Turn away the reproach that I dread,
   for your rules are good.

40 Behold, I long for your precepts;
   in your righteousness give me life!

Three Years

The things of earth will never satisfy.
Only the things of God will fill our hearts.

I opened up the driver's door on the 1980 Cadillac Fleetwood Brougham. The rich burgundy paint on the hood gleamed in the showroom lights. My best friend, Lance Wallbrook, and I were fifteen years old and had just been dropped off by his mom to go look at cars in downtown Atlanta, Georgia.

We got into the vehicle and sat down in the front seats. We had silly grins on our faces as I exclaimed, "Can't beat the smell of a new car, can you? How much does this car retail for?" Lance looked at the sticker price affixed to the passenger window and let out a slow whistle. "Wow! Over forty grand!" For the next forty-five minutes, we went over every detail of this luxury car loaded with premium upgrades.

We left the showroom later that afternoon holding a stack of sleek car booklets. For the next year, I often would open up those brochures and dream of driving in style, but over time I found my interest ebbing.

What is it about new things that captivates the human soul? Why do we yearn for the things of earth to satiate our deepest desires? When you examine the human heart, you find that there is a God-sized hole in us that can only be filled with the presence of our Creator.

> "Turn my eyes from looking at worthless things;
> and give me life in your ways."
>
> Psalm 119:37 ESV

The things of the earth cannot satisfy us. They might for a season give us a measure of delight, but then the new car, gadget, or clothes begin to fade, or even eventually wear out, and we find ourselves empty, yearning for something more. Beloved, only our Father in Heaven can fill us with meaning and purpose. It is only He who can give us peace that surpasses understanding. Your heart becomes alive when you begin to seek the things that are transcendent and everlasting. The Word of God is exactly this. It will never fade; it will never cease.[33]

In 2005, while serving in missions in Bangkok, Thailand, the Lord impressed upon me to store up Psalm 119 in my heart. I thought to myself, If I remember correctly, this chapter is the longest chapter in the Bible. This is going to be a challenge! It turned out to be. It took almost three years of slow, plodding work before I was able to quote the chapter in one sitting. By the time I finished, we had just completed a total of sixteen years of mission work in Thailand and had moved back to the U.S. I quoted it for one of my good friends, and then promptly put it on the shelf. It was not until twelve years later that the Holy Spirit challenged me to pick it up again.

The writer of Psalm 119 has never been disclosed, but many scholars believe that it was King David. I would like to believe that it was, for this reason: David wrote Psalm 19, which is essentially the ancient SparkNotes of Psalm 119. I often imagine David as a shepherd boy out under the stars with his sheep, strumming a harp and singing worship melodies to Yahweh. There are seven synonyms that are used in this chapter to describe the Word of God. Why? What was the purpose of using so many different descriptions of the Torah? The picture that I see is one of a prism that refracts light. When light enters a prism, it splits into the seven visible colors of the spectrum. All these distinct colors make up white light. Each of them is unique,

---

[33] Isaiah 40:8

and each of them is beautiful. Allow these poetic words to flow over your tongue and be planted in your heart.

Over the past five decades, I have grown from a teenage boy infatuated with luxury cars into a man who has gone through many seasons of life, maturing in the ways of God. I am presently getting my "Master's" in the book of Job, battling the giant of ALS. After eight years of going through the fire, Psalm 119 has become part of my daily bread. These words of life are not simply life-giving; they have sustained me through these trials. Beloved, do you understand what I am saying? These words are Jesus. He is the Son of Man who was born in Bethlehem, which in Hebrew means the "House of Bread," and He became the Bread of Life to all mankind.[34] I eat of this Bread every day, and I am more alive than I have ever been in fifty-six years of living. The things of this earth will never satisfy us like the way Jesus satisfies. Selah.

Journal

What things presently captivate your heart that are not eternal?

How can you grow in hunger for spiritual manna that truly satisfies?

Cultivate a heart of gratitude by writing down the things that the Lord has given you. In this place of fresh thankfulness, worship the One who has given us His all.

Prayer

Abba, forgive me when my heart is captivated by the things of this earth. Forgive me when I go after lesser gods. Cleanse my mind and

---

[34] John 6:35 NIV

heart with your love and grace. Fill me with joy eternal that comes from your presence and the indwelling Living Word.

In the Name of Jesus!

Hebrew Treasure
Thomas L. Boehm

ה Hey

How hungry are you for God? Appetites drive actions. This stanza opens with a hungry cry by the Psalmist to learn from Almighty God Himself. He is hungry to engage the Father's heart and to learn from Him. His heart is in a holy posture of openness. He cries out, Horeini (הוֹרֵנִי) — meaning teach me! — a heavenly hungry and open-hearted plea to learn. This word also begins with the Hebrew letter hey (ה). This same word is found in my favorite go-to prayer in Psalm 86:11, "Teach me Your way, Oh Lord, and I will walk in Your truth; Give me an undivided heart to fear Your Name." It is a desperate plea — hungry and open to God — asking not only for information to fill the head but power to unite the heart in whole-hearted surrender and obedience. One of the earliest uses of this root word in Scripture is in Exodus 4:12 when God commissions Moses to lead the Israelites out of slavery. He promises, "I will teach you what to say." Jesus promises His followers the same intimate and relationally driven leadership in John 16:12-15. He promises to "guide/lead/teach you" by the voice of His Holy Spirit. As you work on cultivating a holy appetite of hunger for God and openness to follow His lead, be encouraged — God is the best teacher. His instruction is the only food that will ultimately feed and satisfy you!

Waw - Worship with the Word - "Steadfast Love"
by Mark Woodward

DAY 6
The Psalm 119 Journey

ו

Waw

41 Let your steadfast love come to me, O Lord,
 your salvation according to your promise;

42 Then shall I have an answer for him who taunts me,
 for I trust in your word.

43 And take not the word of truth utterly out of my mouth,
 for my hope is in your rules.

44 I will keep your law continually,
 forever and ever,

45 And I shall walk in a wide place,
 for I have sought your precepts.

46 I will also speak of your testimonies before kings
 and shall not be put to shame,

47 For I find my delight in your commandments,
 which I love.

48 I will lift up my hands toward your commandments, which I
 love, and I will meditate on your statutes.

Conviction

The man or woman of God who trusts the Word,
Will not be put to shame.

The sound of a dozen basketballs bouncing on the wooden court reverberated through the gym as I walked over to the coach's office. Our high school basketball coach was not to be trifled with, and I was nervous for the discussion I was about to have with him.

"Uh…Coach, do you have a minute?" I asked apprehensively.

He looked up, not saying anything, and simply nodded, motioning for me to sit down.

"With basketball practice going for 3-4 hours every day after school, I'm not able to attend youth group at my church on Wednesday nights. I would like your permission to leave an hour early."

Coach crossed his arms and lifted his chin as he began to speak.

"If you're going to play for me, you have got to make basketball a priority, Son."

He paused for seemingly dramatic effect, then cleared his throat and said,

"And by the way, I didn't know you were a Christian."

I felt a sharp stab in my gut as conviction hit me. Wow, I thought to myself. Has my behavior been that unimpressive that he didn't know that I was a follower of Jesus?

"Umm…can I get back with you on that, Coach, in a few days?" I mumbled as I looked down at the floor.

He nodded and went back to his play chart, getting ready for the upcoming Friday night game. I went home that evening and sat down with my folks, and shared what had happened.

"Steve, what's more important to you, basketball or your faith?" my dad asked. I thought for a moment about how much I loved basketball and had dreamed about one day playing in the NBA. The reality was, I was 5'6" and sitting bench.

"My faith is more important, Dad. Basketball is a lot of fun, but I know that it's not my life."

"Then I would make your decision based on your conviction, Son," my dad responded.

Within the next week, I went back to my coach and let him know that I was leaving the team so that I could attend youth group on Wednesday nights and make that my first priority.

Our beliefs rest upon our convictions, and our convictions have consequences. At the age of seventeen, my convictions were tested, and I found that they were worthy of sacrifice. King David later penned these words:

"Let your steadfast love come to me, O Lord,

your salvation according to your promise;

Then shall I have an answer for him who taunts me,

for I trust in your word."

Psalm 119:41-42 ESV

Beloved, do you want to grow in your convictions? Hunger after the Word of God. The Word of God is powerful and active, and has the ability to divide the flesh from the spirit. It is sharp, like a knife, to parse our thoughts and intentions. Growing up, our children, in our family morning devotions, memorized scripture like this proverb:

"Train a child in the way he should go,

and when he is old he will not turn from it."

Proverbs 22:6 NIV 1984

Line by line, and precept by precept, truth grows in our hearts. "Then you will know the truth, and the truth will set you free."[35] Forty-one years ago, I made the decision to stand on my convictions, and I stood up to my basketball coach by choosing youth group over my favorite sport. When you live by the truth, the truth will set you free. Selah.

Journal

Think back to a time in your life when your convictions were tested. What enabled you to stand the test?

---

[35] John 8:32 NIV

What practical ways can you strengthen your convictions this year?

Prayer

Papa, thank You for Your steadfast love, and for Your Word that is eternal. Thank You that my convictions are not based on the tyranny of popular culture, but rather upon the truth of Your love.

In the Name of Jesus!

Hebrew Treasure
Thomas L. Boehm

Waw ו

This 6th stanza of Psalm 119 begins with the word Vi'vo-oo'ni (וִיבֹאֻנִי) which means, And let come to me, and begins with the conjunction waw or vav (ו). In this case, we are focusing on the function rather than the meaning of the Hebrew letter/word. A conjunction is a part of speech that links words, phrases, and clauses. A conjunction, though seemingly small and often overlooked, serves a critical function–linkage. This conjunction is recognizable in a few of these eight verses in English translations, but is hidden in most of them (i.e. and, then). In Hebrew, all eight verses in this stanza do begin with the Hebrew conjunction waw. The conjunction waw links these verses together around the topic of loving God's instructions as the path of relating rightly with God and others. Legalism is toxic, but staying linked to Jesus is transformational. Legalism flourishes when there are rules without right relationship. When Christian community perpetuates a culture of legalism — a counterfeit for what God calls true religion (Ja. 1:27; Col. 2:8) — faith is undermined and love wilts. The antidote for legalism is right relationship with God and walking and working that out in real time with others. And let's be honest — relationships are messy! But God is in the business of cleaning up our mess and Jesus is always the way God does this transformational work. Staying linked to Jesus in right relationship in real time is the antidote to legalism. Psalm 119 is a huge help with this! Beloved, let the written word of God link you to the living Word of God. As you do, you are investing in right relationship with God that will slay legalism and spark the faith needed to love well.

Zayin - Worship with the Word - "Remember Me"
by Mark Woodward

DAY 7
The Psalm 119 Journey

ז

Zayin

49 Remember your word to your servant,
   in which you have made me hope.

50 This is my comfort in my affliction,
   that your promise gives me life.

51 The insolent utterly deride me,
   but I do not turn away from your law.

52 When I think of your rules from of old,
   I take comfort, O Lord.

53 Hot indignation seizes me because of the wicked,
   who forsake your law.

54 Your statutes have been my songs
   in the house of my sojourning.

55 I remember your name in the night, O Lord,
   and keep your law.

56 This blessing has fallen to me,
   that I have kept your precepts.

Firing Squad
The gospel is not only worth living for,
it is worth dying for.

"Ready your rifles!" the executioner barked out to the uniformed soldiers standing at attention a mere fifty yards from the English missionary families who were about to die. The families stood in a long line, almost fifty strong. Children were openly crying while wives clung to their husbands. It was 1900, and the Boxer Revolt was in full swing on the mainland of China. Here in the courtyard of City Hall in Taiyuan, the capital of Shanxi Province, new martyrs were being added to the swelling ranks of those who had gone to meet their Maker. A new emperor had taken power who was rabidly anti-foreigner and anti-missionary. [36]

A large crowd of rowdy townspeople, standing behind the soldiers, jeered and yelled at the missionaries. They had been whipped into a frenzied excitement, coerced by a few strategically placed agitators. Most of them did not know the missionaries, and only had glimpsed the "foreign devils" from a distance in the marketplaces.

A gray-haired missionary in the middle of the line of captives began to sing a hymn, and quickly the song was joined by the families down the line. The townspeople, hearing the earthly choir, grew silent one by one until only the voices of those condemned to die were heard.

"Fire!" the executioner shouted, and the families, mowed down by the slicing bullets, fell lifeless to the ground. Blood ran deep at the feet of the martyrs, their sacrifice watering the harvest of souls that was to come.

"Whoever wants to be my disciple must deny themselves and take up their cross daily and follow me. For whoever wants to save their life will lose it,

---

[36] Graham, Ruth Bell. Legacy of a Pack Rat. Nelsonword Publishing Group, 1994. (Historical accuracy to this story comes from Ruth Graham's chapter titled "The Executioner.")

but whoever loses their life for me will save it."[37]

It was 2005, and my wife, Samantha, my youngest son, Isaiah, and I had flown from the mission field in Bangkok, Thailand, to Beijing, China, and then on to Taiyuan to adopt a two-year-old Chinese girl, whom we named Jezreel. She had been left on the front steps of the state orphanage in Datong City in Shanxi Province. The year before, I had read the story of the missionary massacre in Taiyuan, the capital of Shanxi Province, in the footnoted book of short stories written by Ruth Bell Graham, the wife of Billy Graham. Ruth had grown up in China, the daughter of a missionary family in the '40s, and had an uncle who had survived the Boxer Revolt.

"Honey, this is where it probably happened..." I quietly spoke to Samantha. A sense of reverence came over me as we stood on hallowed ground. We were standing in the middle of the courtyard of City Hall in Taiyuan, where the blood of the missionaries had watered the ground. There was no memorial to mark this spot here on earth, only the testimony of the saints in the great cloud of witnesses. It was the day after we had adopted Jezreel, and we had asked our guide to take us to City Hall. She thought that we were just sightseeing around the city, but instead we were stepping back into revival history.

> "My comfort in my suffering is this:
> Your promise preserves my life."
>
> Psalm 119:50 ESV

There is a fundamental difference between the church in the East and the church in the West. Many of those in the East have experienced persecution and suffering for wearing the Name of Christ. Unfortunately, many in the West have been deceived into thinking that they should not suffer for being a Christian. The coming tribulations of the end times will refine us all, and will separate the sheep from the goats.[38] The psalmist above experienced

---

[37] Luke 9:23-24 NIV
[38] Matthew 25:31-46

suffering and found his comfort in the promises of God. The Lord will preserve our lives, some miraculously in the present age, but to all of us who believe, in the age to come. Many will be martyred and will be greatly honored by our Heavenly Father.

Beloved, is the gospel worth dying for? Did those missionary families who gave their lives over a hundred years ago waste them? After the communist takeover in World War II, China was shut to the outside world for close to thirty years. Many thought that Christianity had been wiped out by the brutal regime of Chairman Mao Zedong. In the 1970s, when the doors swung open to China, visitors were shocked to discover that the underground church was now over fifty million strong.[39] Jesus spoke to Peter these words that have echoed through the annals of time: "Upon this rock, I will build my church, and the gates of Hades will not overcome it."[40] Selah.

Journal

What stories about persecution from the New Testament and the modern day have increased your faith?

How are you preparing your heart for persecution in the days ahead?

What did Jesus mean when He said, "Take up your cross daily and follow Me"?[41]

---

[39] "From the time China was opened to western visitors in 1973 we have heard a growing stream of reports increasing in their excitement, about house churches there. At first, visitors claimed that, against all odds, the house church movement was still intact after 25 years of persecution. After several years, however, the reports became more sanguine. Estimates appeared claiming that there were 30 million authentic Christians meeting in house churches. Later estimates went higher still to 50 million and beyond."
McCallum, Dennis. Watchman Nee and the House Church Movement in China, Dwell Community Church, 2021, https://dwellcc.org/learning/essays/watchman-nee-and-house-church-movement-china.
[40] Matthew 16:15-19 NIV
[41] Luke 9:23 NIV

Prayer

Abba, thank You that You were willing to send your Son into the earth to endure the hostility of man and suffer under great persecution so that we might find true life. Strengthen us daily, that we too would endure the persecution of the enemy in order that those in the darkness would see a great light. Teach us to count our lives not as our own, but Yours.

In the Name of Jesus!

Hebrew Treasure
Thomas L. Boehm

Zayin ז

Our brains are "leaky"; we are often forgetful. God, therefore, regularly calls us to "remember" what He has done in the past to grow our faith that He is trustworthy and good today and in the future. God calls us to remember the deliverance from slavery in Egypt (Ex. 13:3) and the greater deliverance by Messiah's body (1 Cor. 11:24) and blood (1 Cor. 11:25). Beginning with the letter zayin (ז), Z'chor (זכר) is the Hebrew word for "remember" and a form of this word begins three verses in this stanza. Specifically, verse 49 cries out for God to remember His word to the Psalmist while verses 52 and 55 declare what the Psalmist remembers. The opening of verse 52, "When I think of" is a translation of the root word z'chor, calling to mind God's rules or laws. In verse 55, the Psalmist declares his remembrance of God's Name in the night. Some of the earliest instances of z'chor in the Hebrew Bible include God "remembering" Noah (Gen. 8:1), Abraham (19:29), Rachel (30:22), and His covenant with the Patriarchs (Ex. 2:24). The last prophet recorded in the Hebrew Bible includes a call for us to "remember" God's Torah (i.e., law, instruction) in Malachi 4:4. Psalm 119 certainly helps us heed this live-giving instruction!

Heth - Worship with the Word - "My Portion"
by Joseph Maloney

DAY 8
The Psalm 119 Journey

ח

Heth

57 The Lord is my portion;
   I promise to keep your words.

58 I entreat your favor with all my heart;
   be gracious to me according to your promise.

59 When I think on my ways,
   I turn my feet to your testimonies;

60 I hasten and do not delay
   to keep your commandments.

61 Though the cords of the wicked ensnare me,
   I do not forget your law.

62 At midnight I rise to praise you,
   because of your righteous rules.

63 I am a companion of all who fear you,
   of those who keep your precepts.

64 The earth, O Lord, is full of your steadfast love;
   teach me your statutes!

Masada

You have made the mountains, O Lord.
Upon these rocks, You have ordered my steps.

"Dad, you can do this," my son Michael said. It was July 15, 2015, and I was helping to lead a group of twenty college students with Caleb Company for a one-month, transformative experience in the land of Israel. We had left our apartment in the heart of Jerusalem at 4:00 a.m. that morning to drive out into the desert to hike Masada, the iconic mountaintop on which King Herod had built his summer palace two millennia before. [42]

"Thanks, Son. One step at a time, and we'll make it," I said with difficulty between labored breaths. We were halfway up the Snake Trail, which wound steeply up the side of Masada. My two oldest sons, Michael and Kanaan, were on my right and left sides, their arms around me, helping me trek to the top of this rock sentinel that towered over the lowest place on earth, the Dead Sea. Every summer, it was a rite of passage for our ministry students to make this hike before sunrise. It was about a year before, when we had spent a month in Israel during the Gaza War, that I started to experience the first symptoms of ALS with left foot drop. Over the past year, I had begun to use lace-up ankle boots with metal brace inserts to give my feet support, as well as a walking cane. ALS is a neurodegenerative disease, and slowly over time, the muscles atrophy, losing their ability to operate.

---

[42] "The Masada Snake Path is one of the most iconic hikes in Israel. Masada is an ancient and famous fortress that stands beside the dead sea. Starting from the base, the Snake Path winds its way up approximately 400 meters (about ¼ mile) from the lowest place on earth, the Dead Sea. It then continues to the peak. Here, archaeological remains tell a story of heroism and endurance. You can enjoy magnificent views of the Dead Sea and the Moab Mountains of Jordan on the other side. The fortress at Masada was built by King Herod, conquered by a group of Jewish zealots, and was besieged by the Romans soon after. Rather than be captured, the zealots decided to commit suicide, and their story of heroism and courage is recounted to this day." "Masada Snake Path." Tourist Israel, Tourist Israel: The Guide, 1 Aug. 2021, https://www.touristisrael.com/masada-snake-path/9684/.

God speaks to me through mountains. I experience His presence powerfully when I am in His creation and see His handiwork. In my twelve trips to Israel, I have ascended to the top of Masada each time. This time was the most memorable, and the last time in seven years that I was able to go up it on my own two feet.

"I need to take a break," I told my sons as we were within sight of the top of the mountain after ninety minutes of hiking. The rest of our team had already made it to the top and were enjoying the brilliant desert sunrise. Sweat was trickling down the front of my face as I sat on a large rock looking down on the Judaean Desert that sprawled beneath me. I could see the distinct rock outlines of the army camp of the Roman Tenth Legion[43] that had laid siege to this fortress two thousand years before. Light danced on the top of the Dead Sea like diamonds scattered on the surface. It struck me how beautiful a desert could be. God is the quintessential artist. Give Him a blank slate, and He will create stunning vistas.

"Only ten more minutes, Dad, and we're to the top," my son Kanaan exclaimed as he helped me to my feet. He pulled out a bandana and handed the other end to Michael. Using it as a sling, they ran it under my left knee, and we fell into a steady cadence, the boys lifting my leg every other step. Our pace quickened nearing the top, and the Caleb Company team began to clap and cheer as we made the last hundred feet. After a long draft of cool water at the top, we took epic pictures of our group banded together with the morning sun climbing behind us.

---

[43] https://scholarworks.sjsu.edu/cgi/viewcontent.cgi?article=1021&context=hist_pub Roth, Jonathan. "The length of the siege of Masada." Scripta Classica Israelica 14 (1995): 87.

THE PSALM 119 JOURNEY

"You did it, Steve. We're so proud of you," said Heather, one of our student leaders. We were walking across the top of the fortress to the back side of the mountain, where a massive rain cistern had been dug by the Zealots who had fiercely defended this plot of rock during the first century. One by one, we carefully descended the jagged stairs into the empty cistern. We formed a loose circle sitting down and began to sing hymns a cappella, softly at first, and then with a great swell, with full voices. A warmth permeated my being as I felt the tangible presence of the Spirit in this hallowed place.

Beloved, what has been your experience with the presence of Father God? How do you most tangibly encounter Him? I think back often to that pre-dawn hike up Masada with my sons. It was a precious gift given to me by my Heavenly Father. He is Emmanuel, God with us. The Lord has numbered our steps and has ordered our ways. He was the One who put strength in our legs to ascend this mountain of the Lord. As I have meditated, prayed, and decreed Psalm 119 early each morning for the last five months, I have seen the power of God in my life. He has increased my hunger for His living Word, and I am much more aware of His handiwork all around me.

> "When I think on my ways,
> I turn my feet to your testimonies."
>
> Psalm 119:59 ESV

It has been said that we do not read the Word, but that the Word reads us. In the simple journey of storing the Word of God in our hearts daily, the Word has the power to transform us, to change us into the likeness of the Son of God. King David, in the Psalm above, meditates on this truth when he contemplates his life and makes the decision to set his feet on pilgrimage to follow the Lord all the days of his life.

In my own journey of following the Lord, I have encountered many mountains that have brought me closer to the heart of God. In my twelve trips to Masada, I have grown in deeper appreciation not only for His creation, but also for His people. His testimonies have become my daily bread. Selah.

Journal

Upon what mountains have you experienced the presence of the Lord?

As you reflect on your spiritual journey, how have you grown in gratitude for the Word of the Lord?

Prayer

Abba, thank You for the mountains that You have placed in my life, physical and spiritual. Thank You for the rich experiences that you have given me through these journeys of ascent. Open my eyes daily to see fresh evidence of Your handiwork all around me. You are the Creator of all. You are the Giver of all life. Order my steps as I walk in Your ways.

In the Name of Jesus!

Hebrew Treasure

Thomas L. Boehm

Heth ח

Oh, how we long for trustworthy leaders who are both good and powerful. A bad leader cannot be trusted to make good choices that will benefit those being led. A weak leader cannot be trusted to have the ability to execute and deliver on those good choices. God is both totally good and all powerful. Furthermore, His desire has always been to bless His people by leading us through relationships of trust. This trust was broken by Adam, renewed by Abraham, and scaled up through Jesus who restored access — through faith — to God's good leadership beyond the physical descendents of Isaac and Jacob. The Hebrew word chesed, often translated as loving-kindness or goodness, is best translated as covenant-fidelity. God is always faithful and will fulfill all of His promises. The last verse in this stanza opens with Chas-d'cha (חַסְדְּךָ) in which the Psalmist declares to God that His good and powerful leadership — His steadfast love, His covenant-fidelity — fills the earth. This Hebrew word begins with the next letter in the Hebrew alphabet heth (ח). In addition to verse 46, Psalm 119 also points us to God's chesed, His covenant-fidelity in verses 41, 76, 88 (see Hebrew Treasure in chapter 11), 124, 149, and 159. As a child of God, born again through faith in Jesus, you are safe under God's leadership and you can trust Him even when your circumstances don't align with your preferences. Beloved, trust in God's goodness and that even today He is powerfully working all things together for your good!

Teth - Worship with the Word - "Gold and Silver"
by Mark Woodward

DAY 9

The Psalm 119 Journey

ט

Teth

65 You have dealt well with your servant,
   O Lord, according to your word.

66 Teach me good judgment and knowledge,
   for I believe in your commandments.

67 Before I was afflicted I went astray,
   but now I keep your word.

68 You are good and do good;
   teach me your statutes.

69 The insolent smear me with lies,
but with my whole heart I keep your precepts;

70 Their heart is unfeeling like fat,
but I delight in your law.

71 It is good for me that I was afflicted,
   that I might learn your statutes.

72 The law of your mouth is better to me
   than thousands of gold and silver pieces.

Three Days
Three days to number my days.
Three days that shifted my gaze.

Be a good soldier for Jesus, I told myself as I was wheeled out the front door on a gurney. I had been coughing now for four days, and a home health care nurse had dropped by to take my vitals and said I needed to go to the hospital immediately. Today, November 25, 2021, was going to be a number of firsts: first time in an ambulance, first time in the ER, and first time to be deathly sick on Thanksgiving. Two paramedics, John and Cindy, transported me to Memorial North Hospital in Colorado Springs. They were professional and kind in the way that they treated me.

Within a matter of minutes, we were pulling into the back of the ER, where I was taken into a private exam room. I thought that with Thanksgiving, there would be a long wait, but it was the opposite. The room filled up with RNs and an attending ER physician. In less than an hour, after a number of tests, they had diagnosed me with double pneumonia and COVID, a one-two punch that, during the last two years, has sent many elderly to the grave.

I was taken up to the third floor of the hospital and spent the next three days fighting the infection. With COVID restrictions, no family members could visit me. On top of this, my wife had her hands full taking care of our twenty-year-old adopted daughter from China, who was doing poorly because of her heart condition.

"Mr. Allen, would you like the TV on?" one of the nurses asked me while coming into the room.

"No, thank you," I replied, thinking to myself, *This is a great time to spend time with the Lord and meditate on the Word.*

That afternoon I meditated on Psalm 90:12:

"Teach us to number our days aright, that we may gain a heart of wisdom."

I had memorized this Scripture twenty years before on the mission field, but today was the first time that I thought to ask the Lord:

What does it look like to number my days?

I immediately sensed in my spirit His answer:

To number your days is to live each day with wonder, amazement, gratitude, thanksgiving, praise, and worship. If you do this each day, you will gain a heart of wisdom.

A blanket of peace settled over me as I contemplated this revelation. In the face of ALS, every day was a gift. Now in the hospital, every hour was a gift. Interestingly, I had no fear, just a sense that the Father was with me. His name is Emmanuel, "God with us."

During those three days, I had opportunities to minister to the nursing staff and share God's love for them. Later, I ended up doing some mentoring with the husband of one of the nurses. The Lord had me on assignment those three days, to be light and salt to those around me.

It was two weeks later when Lou Engle, the founder of TheCall prayer movement, asked me, "Steve, did you think it was your time?" We were in one of our team prayer meetings. I smiled and responded, "It did cross my mind… but I knew the Lord had other plans."

King David wrote these words three thousand years ago. We do not know his affliction, but we do know that he endured many trials.

> "It is good for me that I was afflicted,
>
> that I might learn your statutes."
>
> Psalm 119:71 ESV

Beloved, the storms of life will come upon you. It's not a matter of "if," but "when." Don't be surprised by the trials that you face. They are a part of a fallen world. In our afflictions, we are humbled and weakened. In this place of weakness, God shows His strength. One of the greatest Christian thinkers of the twentieth century, C.S. Lewis, penned these words on the subject of pain:

"Pain insists upon being attended to. God whispers to us in our pleasures, speaks in our consciences, but shouts in our pains. It is His megaphone to rouse a deaf world."

Beloved, during the three days I spent in the sanctum of that hospital room, I reflected on the past seven years of my journey. I have always had a great love for the Word of God, but the crushing disease of ALS has focused me in such a way that this Word that became flesh has now become my daily bread. I spend at least an hour a day meditating on and memorizing His Word. The more I eat of it, the more my hunger increases. Read the moving words of the ancient prophet, Jeremiah:

> "When your words came, I ate them;
>
> they were my joy and my heart's delight,
>
> for I bear your name,
>
> Lord God Almighty."
>
> Jeremiah 15:16 NIV

May your daily reading of the Word of God be more than a checkpoint for your spiritual to-do list. Instead, may it become your Living Bread. I was given a great gift with the three days I had in the hospital, three days to reflect on all the riches that He had given me. When you learn to number your days, you learn that His Word is life itself. Selah.

Journal

How can a sickness or any other trial recalibrate your focus on what is most important?

How can the Scripture help you to number your days and give you a heart of wisdom?

Prayer

Abba Father, thank You that You did not leave us without Your Words. You did not leave us as orphans. Thank You that Your Words are life. These Words fill us with hope eternal, joy unceasing, and love unfailing.

In the Name of Jesus!

Hebrew Treasure

Thomas L. Boehm

Teth ט

Do you like to suffer or be afflicted? Of course not! No one does. But God's ways are higher than ours and our call as followers of Jesus is to walk by faith, and in all our ways to acknowledge God (i.e., bear witness to His goodness) rather than to walk by sight and to lean on our own understanding (2 Cor. 5:7; Prov. 3:5-6). Our primary challenge in this Age could be summarized simply as learning to eat from the right tree — the Tree of Life — free from the curse of the Fall (Gen. 2-3). The alternative, woven deeply into the fabric of fallen flesh, is an instinct to trust in ourselves and eat from the Tree of the Knowledge of Good and Evil. The Hebrew word for "good" is tov (טוֹב), beginning with the letter teth(ט), and a form of this word is used six times in this stanza. Specifically, it is translated well in verse 65, it's translated good in verses 66, 68 (twice), and 71, and is translated better in verse 72. Furthermore, whereas "goodness" is ascribed as a trait or attribute of God in verses 65, 68 (twice), and 72, David uses this word to describe how God has treated him in verse 66. In verse 71 David uses this word to describe the value of his own affliction and the suffering that resulted. Now this is shocking. Suffering is good?! Reread verse 71. How can this be? Well, David provides the answer in verse 67 when he explains the good fruit from his bad circumstances. Before he was afflicted, David says he went astray. The word translated affliction in verses 67 and 71 is indeed the same Hebrew word. Perhaps David realizes his tendency — just like ours — to lean on our own understanding, walk by sight, and stumble as a result (just read Psalm 51 for another example of David describing his stumbling and turning after the debacle with Bathsheba!). This stumbling or going astray in verse 67 is contrasted with David's ongoing commitment to keep or obey God's Word. Beloved, even in your difficult or unpleasant circumstances, God is good, He is for you, and He is working all things together for your tov (good; Rom. 8:28)! Trust Him and don't let go of your faith — He will never let go of you!

Don't give up hope because God's love is surely better than life (Ps. 63:3). Jesus overcame death so you can be with Him and experience His tov-ness, His goodness, forever.

Yodh - Worship with the Word - "Maker"
by Mark Woodward

DAY 10
The Psalm 119 Journey

׳

Yodh

73 Your hands have made and fashioned me;
   give me understanding that I may learn your commandments.

74 Those who fear you shall see me and rejoice,
   because I have hoped in your word.

75 I know, O Lord, that your rules are righteous,
   and that in faithfulness you have afflicted me.

76 Let your steadfast love comfort me
   according to your promise to your servant.

77 Let your mercy come to me, that I may live;
   for your law is my delight.

78 Let the insolent be put to shame,
   because they have wronged me with falsehood;
   as for me, I will meditate on your precepts.

79 Let those who fear you turn to me,
   that they may know your testimonies.

80 May my heart be blameless in your statutes,
   that I may not be put to shame!

County Jail

The gift of the Law is that it led us to Jesus.
Jesus introduced us to grace.

The metal door swung behind me and shut with a loud clang. A group of men who were playing cards at a small community table swung around to look at who the newcomer was. It was my first time in the St. Louis County Jail as a pastoral volunteer. I was fresh out of college, barely 22, and easily could have passed for a Boy Scout. I was carrying my Bible and wearing a freshly printed name tag.

"Who are you?" asked a salty-looking inmate with a cigarette dangling out of his lips.

"I'm…Steve," I stuttered in a higher-pitched voice than I cared to make.

"What are you playing?" I asked the inmates.

"Spades," responded my soon-to-be friend, whom I will call "Salty."

Within a few minutes I found myself talking to these men who had been waiting for trial, some for upwards of two to three years. Over the next few weeks, I found out Salty's story. A Vietnam vet, he had been wounded and had become addicted to morphine to cope with the intense pain. When he returned to the U.S., he fell in with the wrong crowd and was an accomplice in a bank robbery.

"I wish I could do it over," Salty reflected with a faraway look in his eye. I sat across the table from him, the words hitting me hard. For the next hour, he shared about his upbringing, his carousing high school days, and being drafted into the Army. He was sent halfway around the world to a country that he could barely pronounce, to a people whose language confused him.

I don't remember Salty saying much about his father, which spoke volumes. According to recent statistics, 85% of incarcerated youth do not have fathers in their home.[44]

Over the next two years, I would meet with Salty weekly, sharing with him the life of Jesus and praying with him. He was tried and given twenty years in a maximum-security prison down in Pacific, Missouri. The visits became monthly as I would drive an hour southwest of St. Louis to see him. One of the most sobering messages from Salty's life was his remorse for choosing drugs, and then crime, to try to alleviate his pain and fix his problems. A year later, my wife and I left for the mission field in Southeast Asia and only heard from him sporadically through letters over the next five years. He went up for parole several times but was denied because he had not served enough time.

Beloved, decisions carry consequences. Sin requires payment. One of my spiritual fathers, Don Finto, shared this several years ago:

"Sin will always take you down a path that makes you stay much longer than you intended to stay, pay much more than you intended to pay, and go farther than you intended to go." The psalmist shared these oracles of truth three thousand years ago:

> "I know, O Lord, that your rules are righteous,
> and that in faithfulness you have afflicted me.
> Let your steadfast love comfort me
> according to your promise to your servant."
>
> Psalm 119:75-76 ESV

---

[44] 63% of youth suicides are from fatherless homes (U.S. Dept. Of Health/Census) – 5 times the average. 90% of all homeless and runaway children are from fatherless homes – 32 times the average. 85% of all children who show behavior disorders come from fatherless homes – 20 times the average (Center for Disease Control). 80% of rapists with anger problems come from fatherless homes – 14 times the average (Justice & Behavior, Vol. 14, p. 403-26). 71% of all high school dropouts come from fatherless homes – 9 times the average (National Principals Association Report). Canfield, Ken R. "The Extent of Fatherlessness." National Center for Fathering, 5 Apr. 2022, https://fathers.com/statistics-and-research/the-extent-of-fatherlessness/.

Why are prisons necessary? It is because of the fallen nature of man. The first Adam sinned and bore the consequences of that sin—death. Why is the Law necessary? It is necessary because it shows us our complete depravity without the Promise. The Law is a guardian that leads us to Christ.[45] Salty ended up in jail for breaking the law. All of us have been confronted with our own sin and our inability to keep the complete Law. All of us have broken the Law and have fallen short of His glory.[46]

The Law, like a stern schoolmaster, illuminates our duplicity and exposes us. Thank God that it does not end there. In His great mercy for us, God sent the Man of Reconciliation to bring us back into relationship with the Father. Jesus the Perfect One, our Elder Brother, paid our penalty for breaking the law, on the cross of Calvary.

In my self-justification, I might have said in the past, God, I'm not like those murderers, rapists, and drug sellers that I met in county jail. In response, the Spirit quietly speaks to my heart, Steve, have you ever had thoughts of murder, lust, and greed in your heart? Absolutely. I am not innocent of guilt. The Law leads me to the foot of the cross, and the cross introduces me to grace, and in this grace I am freed.

The psalmist says above, "Let your steadfast love comfort me according to your promise to your servant." We have been the recipients of the fruit of the Promise, which is forgiveness, peace, and comfort. Psalm 119 is a magnificent work of art, the Word of God shown in its glory, grace written on the canvas of life. The Law and the prophets led us to the Word, and the Word became flesh and made His dwelling among us.[47]

Beloved, I encourage you to honor the Law but fully embrace the cross of Christ.[48] No man can keep the Law on his own. It is only through the

---

[45] Galatians 3:23-24
[46] Romans 3:23
[47] John 1:14 NIV
[48] Matthew 5:17-20 NIV

Word and the Spirit that we find the path of freedom. Rejoice today in that revelation.

Journal

Why is the Law so important for us to understand grace?

How does grace introduce you to a true "fear of the Lord"?

What would it look like for you to live in total freedom this year?

Prayer

Father God, we all deserve the penalty of sin, which is death. Thank You that You died on our behalf, that we might embrace true life, and ultimately eternal life. May my life be a symphony of praise for all that You have done for me. Free at last, free at last, thank God I'm free at last.

In the Name of Jesus!

Hebrew Treasure
Thomas L. Boehm

Yodh י

"The informational is transformational only when it is relational." This simple phrase has helped me for decades to wrestle with deeper truths about the importance of relationships over tasks. Relationships are foundational to a life of flourishing. Furthermore, because we are human beings — not human knowings or human doings — our identity needs to be anchored in God and mediated through our relationship with His Son, the Messiah. Relating rightly with God and others is therefore foundational for transformation and growth and this requires knowing God, not just knowing about God. Verse 75 offers a compelling, but complexifying, invitation to look beyond the informational to the relational. Specifically, it forces us to look squarely in the face of our own affliction and suffering and contend with our understanding of our circumstances (which we cannot always control) and our reactions (which are under our control). This requires not only thinking rightly, but can push us to the deeper level of knowing and relating rightly to a sovereign God amidst our circumstances. The Hebrew word for "to know" is yadah and begins with the letter yodh (י). David opens verse 75 with the word Ya-da'ti (יָדַעְתִּי). This word begins with the smallest Hebrew letter yodh and David uses this word to describe his "knowing" two things. First, God's judgments or rules are righteous. Second, David's afflictions somehow flow from God's faithfulness. Now, put aside for a moment the nagging question of whether God is the author of evil. This question is often a distraction from going deeper than merely seeking right thinking about God with right information to a deeper and more transformational wrestling for relating rightly with God. Flourishing in your relationship with God requires a faith-filled heart of surrender and submission to His higher ways which is not easy…but it is good (tov). This same root verb yadah, to know, is used in Exodus 2:25. The English Standard Version captures the Hebrew well, "God saw the people of Israel — and God (yadah) knew." Other translations add qualifying words that point to what God knew but the Hebrew points to God's intimate and relational engagement. This deepest level of "knowing" is clearly seen in the way this same word is used to refer to having sexual relations. Genesis 4:1 describes Adam "knowing" Eve in a most holy and intimate way, not just knowing about her or only having access to information about her. He knew her. It is this same deeper level of knowing that Jesus describes in John 17 when He prays for us to know each other and to know Him so we could all be one with, and truly know, our Heavenly Father. Beloved, let your afflictions, and your joys, drive you deeper into the arms of the One who knows you best and loves you most!

Kaph - Worship with the Word - "A Longing Soul"
by Mark Woodward

DAY 11

The Psalm 119 Journey

כ

Kaph

81 My soul longs for your salvation;
   I hope in your word.

82 My eyes long for your promise;
   I ask, "When will you comfort me?"

83 For I have become like a wineskin in the smoke,
   yet I have not forgotten your statutes.

84 How long must your servant endure?
   When will you judge those who persecute me?

85 The insolent have dug pitfalls for me;
   they do not live according to your law.

86 All your commandments are sure;
   they persecute me with falsehood; help me!

87 They have almost made an end of me on earth,
   but I have not forsaken your precepts.

88 In your steadfast love give me life,
   that I may keep the testimonies of your mouth.

Turtle Island

The decisions of those in the world impact us,
But they do not rule or enslave us.

"COME ON!" shouted my best friend, Russ, who was standing at the front of a speedboat; we were riding from the southern coast of Thailand out to Koh Tao—"Turtle Island." Russ and I, as well as two summer mission interns, were out to scuba dive at one of the European backpacking crowd's favorite diving sites in Southeast Asia. The natural beauty and the cheap prices were a dynamic duo that was hard to beat.

The surface of the ocean was choppy that day, with high winds; Russ had to hold onto the front of the boat to keep from being thrown backward as we slammed into the waves. I looked around the bow of the boat at a number of tourists, and then finally locked eyes with Jared and Luke; they had big grins on their faces. All of us were excited about the adventure we were heading into that weekend. We had been planning this for about three months and finally had found time to get away from our busy ministry schedules. We had found a weekend deal that was surprisingly inexpensive. Our beachfront bungalows were about ten dollars a night, and for sixty-five dollars, we were able to purchase an introductory scuba diving package that included one hour of instruction and two dives, which was perfect for our missionary budgets. Looking back later, we should have recognized that the cheap prices concealed something.

After a rough but exhilarating two-hour boat ride out to Turtle Island, we grabbed our backpacks and found a Tuk-Tuk, a three-wheeled open-air taxi. Piling in, we drove around the outer island road, and within fifteen minutes, we were at our small and quaint resort. After checking in at the front desk, we dropped off our packs at our bungalows and went off to meet our Australian scuba diving instructor; he was about the same age as our interns, nineteen years old.

"G'day, Mate," Jack,[49] our new Aussie friend, exclaimed. He was bare-chested and wearing surfing board shorts that were as bright as his personality. We spent the next hour going over the scuba diving gear and what to expect for our first dive the next morning. I was a little surprised at how casual everything was but thought to myself, Well, you get what you pay for.

We spent the rest of the afternoon snorkeling right off the beach in turquoise waters, enjoying the marine life and the natural beauty of this pristine island. Dinner that night was simple fried rice but eaten out of a scooped-out pineapple, which made it fun to eat and helped merit the label "Exotic Island Foods" that was on our stained laminated menu. After dinner, we sat on some lounge chairs on the beach, watching the stunning sunset and telling stories from our youth.

We were a little alarmed when we saw Jack and a handful of his European island friends heading down the beach with bottles of whiskey in their hands, evidently off on their own island excursion. We fell asleep that night with the sound of surf gently lapping the seashore, yards from our front door.

The next morning we were up early to have time with the Lord, reading the Word and worshiping, feeling God's presence in this remote natural preserve. Jack had told us to meet him at the dock at 8:00 a.m. sharp, but when we arrived, he was not there. The Thai crew, who was very familiar with the drill, was loading up scuba gear and supplies for the day's outing. I struck up a conversation with one of the Thai boatmen and asked him where Jack was. The man smiled and said, "Oh, he'll be here eventually." At around 8:20 a.m., Jack came trotting down the dock and jumped into the boat, apologizing profusely. "Sorry mates, it was a short night and I overslept." From the bloodshot eyes and the grey tone of his face, we put two and two together. Within minutes, we had pulled away from the dock and were

---

[49] Not his real name.

headed down the coast to a nearby lagoon, where we would have our first dive. Laying anchor in the untouched cove, we put on our dive suits, scuba gear, masks, and then finally our flippers.

"Now remember, team, when we are down at the bottom, don't surface too quickly or you'll get the bends," reiterated Jack. He continued, "If you need anything, signal me, and I will come help you out."

Sitting on the side of the wooden fishing boat with our backs to the water, we tipped backward into the serene ocean. We bobbed on the surface, as each of us adjusted our masks before descending into the underwater realm. Schools of fish drifted slowly by us as we swam downward toward a large outcropping of boulders. We stayed in loose formation about ten feet apart from each other. Time seemed to be suspended. I was amazed at the varied marine life: stingrays, large groupers, small sharks, and my favorite, the clownfish.

After forty-five minutes, Jack made the signal to start making our way upward. At that time, my mask started to fill up with water, and I frantically motioned for Jack to assist me. He swam over, still hungover, and pulled the mask from my face in an attempt to clear it, but instead my eyes filled with salt water. I panicked and tried to shoot to the surface, but Jack held one of my arms to keep me from going up too quickly. He pushed the mask back up against my face to seal it, but still it was filled with water. I was trying not to hyperventilate by breathing in too quickly, remembering the instructions from the previous afternoon during our "comprehensive introductory session" on the beach. After what seemed like an eternity, and gulping in several mouthfuls of salt water, we broke the surface with me gasping for air.

"You alright, Mate?" Jack asked me, looking the most concerned I had seen him in the last twenty-four hours. I said nothing, as I was still trying to catch my breath. My head throbbed after the rapid change in pressure. "I think

I'll go rest," I said to Jack, and within minutes I was alongside the boat, and the Thai crew pulled me aboard and helped me out of my gear. I ended up spending the rest of the morning at the bow of the trawler, watching the rest of my teammates continue scuba diving as I nursed a pounding headache. Although I ended up snorkeling later that afternoon at another beautiful lagoon, it was the last time I ever went scuba diving. I had learned a valuable lesson: Cheap excursions usually mean, "Go at your own risk."

Beloved, have you noticed that life is a risk? There are no guarantees that we will be insulated from trouble and hardship. My interaction with Jack is probably one that many have had with those in the world. His cavalier attitude toward life and his hangover from the night before almost cost me my life. We are to be in the world but not of the world.[50] Does this mean that I avoid adventure? No. It simply means that my hope and security are not in man or this world, but in my Heavenly Father. King David wrote these words:

> "The insolent have dug pitfalls for me;
>
> they do not live according to your law."
>
> Psalm 119:85 ESV

I am eternally grateful to the Father, that He never sleeps nor slumbers.[51] He has placed angels in watch over me.[52] He has determined my lifespan

---

[50] Do not love the world or the things in the world. If anyone loves the world, the love of the Father is not in him. For all that is in the world—the desires of the flesh and the desires of the eyes and pride of life—is not from the Father but is from the world. And the world is passing away along with its desires, but whoever does the will of God abides forever. I John 2:15-17 ESV

[51] He will not let your foot be moved; he who keeps you will not slumber. Behold, he who keeps Israel will neither slumber nor sleep. Psalm 121:3-4 ESV

[52] Are they not all ministering spirits sent out to serve for the sake of those who are to inherit salvation? Hebrews 1:14 ESV

and the plans that He has for me.[53] We live in a fallen world, with the consequences of the fallen. What makes us any different? We have been blood-bought by Jesus, the King of Kings. We have been redeemed and given a new nature. We no longer live as the world lives, but as glorified sons of the Living God. Our hope is not in this world, but in the One who gives hope evermore. It was God who saved me from drowning off of Turtle Island. It is Yahweh who has kept me every day since that day. Every breath that I breathe is authored by Him. Praise His Name.

Journal

When was a time in your life that you faced a near-death experience? What happened? How did God protect you?

Reflect on this quote by Stephen Mansfield: "Men who believe in eternal life seldom fear death in this life."[54] How has your faith given you freedom to live life to the full?

Prayer

Father God, thank You that You always watch over me and protect me from the schemes of the enemy. Thank You that You came to give me life, and life to the full. May my daily decisions reflect that thanksgiving.

In the Name of Jesus!

---

[53] For I know the plans I have for you, declares the Lord, plans for welfare and not for evil, to give you a future and a hope. Then you will call upon me and come and pray to me, and I will hear you. You will seek me and find me, when you seek me with all your heart. Jeremiah 29:11-13 ESV

[54] From the biography on the life of Winston Churchill, Never Give Up, by Stephen Mansfield.

Hebrew Treasure

Thomas L. Boehm

Kaph כ

Years ago I went through a season of unemployment that was excruciating. At the time, I was married with multiple children and I experienced intense agony over how I would provide for my family. God taught me to trust Him in that season more deeply than if my circumstances were more comfortable and I was in a cushy job. In this stanza, David describes his intense sense of agony amidst his many difficult circumstances. Specifically, his soul is longing for God's salvation (v. 81) and his eyes are longing for God's promised comfort (v. 82). He describes his experience of unrelenting persecution requiring incredible endurance (v. 84). He needed this endurance because people have been trying to trip or entrap him (v. 85, lit. "dug pitfalls") and persecuting him with lies (v. 86, lit. "falsehood"). In fact, his persecution is so intense he feels like he is going to die (v. 87). David must have been experiencing a lot of agony! In the last verse of this stanza, the Psalmist gathers up all this agony and places it at God's feet. In verse 88, David prays for reviving life according to God's covenant fidelity (Hebrew: chesed). Earlier in chapter 8, we looked at the Hebrew word, chesed, that points to God's good and powerful leadership and begins with the Hebrew letter Heth. Here in verse 88, David writes K'chas-d'cha (כְּחַסְדְּךָ). This is the same root word here in verse 88 as earlier in verse 64 but with the Hebrew letter kaph (כ) attached to the front of the word. This letter kaph at the beginning of the word serves as a preposition. As a preposition, kaph means like, as, or according to. As a part of speech, prepositions show a relationship between two things. Here, David uses this small preposition to illustrate his heartfelt desire for a correspondence between two things: his struggling life and God's good leadership. He is trying to hitch his agony and great need onto God's good and powerful leadership. David uses a simple preposition to help him prayerfully and pleadingly cry out for his agony to better align with God's goodness so he can obey the words of God's mouth. Where are you experiencing a sense of agony in your life right now?

Try praying like David by trusting in God's chesed, His good and powerful leadership, to guide you and revive you according to His covenant fidelity and your ultimate blessing!

Lamedh - Worship with the Word - "God of Generations"
by Joseph Maloney

DAY 12
The Psalm 119 Journey

ל

Lamedh

89 Forever, O Lord, your word
   is firmly fixed in the heavens.

90 Your faithfulness endures to all generations;
   you have established the earth, and it stands fast.

91 By your appointment they stand this day,
   for all things are your servants.

92 If your law had not been my delight,
   I would have perished in my affliction.

93 I will never forget your precepts,
   for by them you have given me life.

94 I am yours; save me,
   for I have sought your precepts.

95 The wicked lie in wait to destroy me,
   but I consider your testimonies.

96 I have seen a limit to all perfection,
   but your commandment is exceedingly broad.

Prayer is Life
It is the very air we breathe.
May it fill our lungs.

Briskly rubbing her hands together, my mother remarked, "Boy, it's freezing this morning, isn't it, Isaiah?" as she walked into the small living room.

My twelve-year-old son, Isaiah, was sitting on the hearth in front of the gas fireplace, trying to get warm on that cold February morning.

"How did you sleep, Grandmother?" Isaiah asked as he yawned.

"I slept great," Grandmother Allen replied, as she stepped onto the hearth, standing above Isaiah. As they talked, Grandmother Allen reached for the low ceiling to steady herself. Her hand slipped. Falling, she reached back to grab the mantle. Unknown to us all, since we had only been in the rental house for six months, the mantle was not secured but was simply sitting on top of three angle irons.

"OH NO!" Grandmother yelled as the heavy mantle toppled off its perch and struck Isaiah's head and back.

"OWWW!" Isaiah let out a bloodcurdling yell as he was hurled face-forward onto the middle of the living-room floor. Blood oozed out of the gash on his head as family members rushed into the room to see what had happened. My wife, Samantha, told him to lie still, not sure if his spine had been injured. Within fifteen minutes, paramedics arrived, strapped him down to a stretcher, and sped him off to the local hospital.

At that same time, I was 8,300 miles away in Dacca, the capital of Bangladesh, prayer-walking on the rooftop of a guest house. It was my third trip there in nine months, as I was working with a missions organization doing leadership training with a rapidly multiplying house church movement. Each night before bed, I would go to the rooftop to pray for my family, intercede for the lost, and worship. I would often feel the presence of the Lord with me as I sought His face. The next morning, Samantha called me to tell me what happened. I was relieved to hear that Isaiah's only lingering souvenirs were three butterfly stitches on top of his head.

Is prayer important? Does it really make a difference if we intercede for our family and for those around us? Absolutely. Jesus taught us to pray in Matthew 6 of the Beatitudes:

> "This, then, is how you should pray:
> 'Our Father in heaven,
> hallowed be your name,
> your kingdom come,
> your will be done,
> on earth as it is in heaven.
> Give us today our daily bread.
> And forgive us our debts,
> as we also have forgiven our debtors.
> And lead us not into temptation,
> but deliver us from the evil one.'"
>
> Matthew 6:9-13 NIV

How many times have we been spared from tragedy without our knowledge? God has placed angels in watch over us.[55] Prayer is faith in action. It is speaking the Living Word back to the Father.

> "If your law had not been my delight,
> I would have perished in my affliction."
>
> Psalm 119:92 ESV

Looking back on that night nine years ago, I am deeply moved that God heard my prayers for my family and spared Isaiah from lasting injury. The enemy is here to kill, steal, and destroy…but God. For the last decade, every morning I pray The Lord's Prayer as a decree over my family. The Word of

---

[55] Hebrews 1:14

God is living and active, sharper than any two-edged sword.[56] Beloved, take up the Word of God. Pray His Word back to the Father and see the hand of God at work in your family and daily life. Make the Word of God your delight. Store the Word of God in your heart. Pray the Word of God each and every day. Selah.

Journal

What have you learned about the nature of God from prayer?

How have you used the Living Word of God in prayer?

What is one thing that you can do this week that will grow your prayer life?

Prayer

Papa, thank You for Your protection over my life and the lives of my family and those I love. You have kept us from the enemy's grasp more times than I will ever know this side of eternity. You are faithful, God. You will never leave us, nor forsake us. I worship You. I love You Abba.

In the Name of Jesus!

Hebrew Treasure
Thomas L. Boehm

Lamedh ל

My father used to tell me "always and never are two words you should always remember never to use." He was being silly, of course, but the point is that always and never are significant words. They are filled with absoluteness; they point beyond the limits of time. David uses similar words in this stanza in both verses 89 and 93. In verse 89, he describes God's word as always being

---

[56] Hebrews 4:12a ESV

firmly fixed in the heavens. In verse 93, he describes never forgetting God's precepts. In both of these verses, however, David uses the same Hebrew word, L'olam (לְעוֹלָם), beginning with the letter lamedh (ל), to express these absolute timeless, or "time-full" concepts. In verse 89, God's word is absolutely fixed in the heavens forever. In verse 93, David's remembrance of God's words are fixed in his memory forever. Genesis 1:1 says, "In the beginning, God created the heavens and the earth." These two realms, heaven and earth, respectively, are the backdrop for David's two assertions. In the first case, David asserts that God's words are fixed in the heavens. In the second case, David asserts that his commitments on earth include a timeless allegiance to God's precepts. This allegiance is expressed through David's commitment to remember God's word that seems designed to anchor the reality of heaven here on earth through David's life and leadership. The first biblical instance of l'olam is in Genesis 3:22. In the Garden, immediately after the original deception and disobedience, God said, "Behold, the man has become like one of us in knowing good and evil. Now, lest he reach out his hand and take also of the tree of life and eat, and live forever." Beloved, we were created for eternity and those surrendered and submitted to the Messiah will live l'olam (forever) in God's presence when the Kingdom of God comes fully here on earth as it already is in heaven.

Mem - Worship with the Word - "Man of Wisdom"
by Joseph Maloney

DAY 13

The Psalm 119 Journey

מ

Mem

97 Oh how I love your law!
   It is my meditation all the day.

98 Your commandment makes me wiser than my enemies,
   for it is ever with me.

99 I have more understanding than all my teachers,
   for your testimonies are my meditation.

100 I understand more than the aged,
   for I keep your precepts.

101 I hold back my feet from every evil way,
   in order to keep your word.

102 I do not turn aside from your rules,
   for you have taught me.

103 How sweet are your words to my taste,
   sweeter than honey to my mouth!

104 Through your precepts I get understanding;
   therefore I hate every false way.

Tsunami

The pleasures of life
Pale in comparison to eternity.

"I was standing in front of a counter with rows of delicious donuts, trying to decide which one I wanted to buy," my best friend, Russ, shared. He was recounting a dream to about a hundred Thai friends and neighbors at our annual Christmas outreach. It was Sunday evening, December 26th, 2004, and our mission team and Thai church had been praying for three months to see friends come to the Lord. Russ continued with his dream, "As I became aware of my surroundings, I noticed that I was in a donut shop on a beachfront. I looked behind me, and off the shore I saw a massive wave rushing toward me. I intuitively knew that this was a tsunami and would be incredibly destructive. I felt myself in the dream caught in the tension between two realms: the physical state of wanting to buy a really delicious donut and the spiritual reality that the coast was about to be wiped out, and many would lose their lives. At that moment the Holy Spirit spoke to me, Russ, you're more concerned with your own hunger than the fact that many are about to perish eternally."

The crowd was spellbound as they listened to Russ share his dream, as news that afternoon had reached us in Bangkok that southern Thailand had been hit hard by a tsunami; they were estimating thousands dead. Russ then gave a simple but unforgettable presentation of the Gospel, inviting those listening to give their lives to Jesus. A number of hands went up and prayed with Russ to receive Jesus into their hearts. I have never forgotten that night, now eighteen years ago, and its powerful reminder for me to share the Gospel.

In the weeks ahead, we learned that over 230,000 people had perished in the Indian Ocean tsunami that destroyed coastal regions of five nations.[57] Our

---

[57] "The 2004 Indian Ocean tsunami, one of the deadliest disasters in modern history, was caused by a massive undersea earthquake. Nearly 230,000 people died, and millions more lost everything. World Vision raised more than $350 million and mounted the largest disaster response in its history, providing relief and

mission team traveled down to Phuket in Southern Thailand to minister in Muslim fishing villages where both homes and families had been destroyed. We shared Jesus as we helped clean up dwellings.

"When the big wave hit, our home quickly filled with water, and I had to make the decision on whether to save my blind father or my special needs son," the fisherman shared with great emotion. "I decided to save my son, and the next day I found my father's body covered by debris and palm branches in the field hundreds of yards from our house." We gave the man bags of rice and cans of food that would last him a few weeks as he and the rest of his family recovered from the catastrophe. He allowed us to pray for them in the Name of Jesus as we asked God to comfort their family in this great loss and reveal to them the love of His Son.

Beloved, Russ's dream convicted me that I am often focused on my own desires rather than the needs of the lost around me. Over the last decade, as I have pursued the Spirit of God and the Word of God in my life, I have grown in my joy of sharing Jesus with others. Jeremiah the prophet said, "When your words came, I ate them; they were my joy and my heart's delight."[58] When we take the Word of God into our hearts, we are eating of Living Bread, and this Living Bread is the Bread of Life for all mankind. Allow the Spirit of God and the Word of God to transform your heart to see the Kingdom treasure all around you–the souls of men that will perish unless we speak. King David penned these words three thousand years ago:

---

rehabilitation in Indonesia, Sri Lanka, Thailand, India, and Myanmar over 10 years." Reid, Kathryn. "2004 Indian Ocean Earthquake and Tsunami: Facts, Faqs, and How to Help." World Vision, World Vision, 4 June 2020, https://www.worldvision.org/disaster-relief-news-stories/2004-indian-ocean-earthquake-tsunami-facts

[58] Jeremiah 15:16a NIV

> "How sweet are your words to my taste,
>
> sweeter than honey to my mouth!"
>
> Psalm 119:103 ESV

There is something sweeter than donuts, and that is the Word of God. That Word became flesh and dwelt among us.[59] Christ in us is the hope of glory,[60] not only for ourselves, but for the lost around us. Russ's dream led to a Gospel presentation that saw Thais coming to Christ. Out of devastation, new life arose.

Journal

What friends and family do you have that are lost and are seeking truth?

Start by praying for them by name for the next thirty days, asking the Holy Spirit to open up opportunities to share Jesus with them.

As they come to Christ, write your testimonies down and share them with other believers to help ignite their faith.

---

[59] John 1:14 NIV
[60] Colossians 1:27 NIV

Prayer

Abba Father, thank You that You have rescued me from the dominion of darkness and have brought me into the Kingdom of the Son You love.[61] Let my life be a response of gratitude for God's grace, by helping to rescue those who are in the tsunami of satan's rage.

In the Name of Jesus!

Hebrew Treasure
Thomas L. Boehm

Mem מ

When the Hebrew letter mem (מ) is at the beginning of a word it functions as a preposition and is translated from. Mem is also the first letter of the Hebrew word, mish'pat, translated as judgment, justice, rule, or ordinance. Psalm 119:102 starts with both the preposition mem and the Hebrew word mish'pat. Thus, this first word of verse 102 is Mi-mish'pa-teicha (מִמִּשְׁפָּטֶיךָ) that is made up of both the preposition mem and the Hebrew word mish'pat but also includes a 2nd person singular pronoun, cha, at the end that is translated your and makes it about God's ordinances. Together, the translation of Mi-mish'pa-teicha is David telling God he will not turn aside from Your rules (or from Your judgments or from Your ordinances). David is committed to allegiance to walking in God's ways and obeying God's words. This allegiance to God's mish'pat (plural is mish'patim) can be seen in his using the word mish'pat a total of 23 times in Psalm 119 alone. Specifically, David uses mish'pat 11 times earlier in verses 7, 13, 20, 30, 39, 43, 52, 62, 75, 84, and 91. Additionally, he uses it 11 times later in psalm 119 in verses 106, 108, 120, 121, 132, 137, 149, 156, 160, 164, and 175. This

---

[61] Colossians 1:13-14 NIV

biblical word shows up for the very first time in the Bible in Genesis 18:19. Specifically, God uses it to explain how the children of Abraham will receive His blessings by "keeping the Way of the LORD" by which He means "doing righteousness and mish'pat (justice)". The prophet Micah echoes this call to do justice using this same Hebrew word mish'pat when he answers the question of "[W]hat does the LORD require of you?" He answers this question, "to do mish'pat, to love chesed (mercy or covenant fidelity), and to walk humbly with your God" (Micah 6:8). Our sense of justice is too often defined by what we feel is right rather than what God has decreed by His word. Let's commit ourselves today to doing mish'pat through faith-fueled obedience in the power of God's Spirit.

Nun - Worship with the Word - "The Lamp"
by Mark Woodward

DAY 14
The Psalm 119 Journey

נ

Nun

105 Your word is a lamp to my feet
   and a light to my path.

106 I have sworn an oath and confirmed it,
   to keep your righteous rules.

107 I am severely afflicted;
   give me life, O Lord, according to your word!

108 Accept my freewill offerings of praise, O Lord,
   and teach me your rules.

109 I hold my life in my hand continually,
   but I do not forget your law.

110 The wicked have laid a snare for me,
   but I do not stray from your precepts.

111 Your testimonies are my heritage forever,
   for they are the joy of my heart.

112 I incline my heart to perform your statutes
   forever, to the end.

The Hand of God

Peace is not the absence of conflict.
Rather, it is the presence of God.

I stood there stunned, listening to the testimony of the two female Orthodox students who were studying at a midrasha,[62] as they excitedly recounted reading a front-page news article from the morning edition of The Times of Israel. Our mission team comprised of college students from Caleb Company in Tennessee was in the middle of Jerusalem, at Teddy Park. We were hosting a barbecue and inviting passers-by to join us so that we could get to know each other and discuss culture, history, and beliefs.

The day before, our team had gone down to Ashdod on the coast to meet with a Russian Jewish pastor and his staff. He wanted to take us to visit an Iron Dome missile defense installation on the outskirts of town. He told us that he was not sure that we could get in to talk to the soldiers, but that we would try. We stopped by a local grocery store and loaded up with snacks, soda, and toiletries for the young soldiers. When our five-car caravan pulled up to the chain link fence outside of the small base, two Israeli soldiers, one male and one female, with loaded machine guns, started walking toward us with their hands stretched out, signaling us to stop.

"Shalom!" said our fearless leader, the pastor, as he stepped out of the lead car with a beaming smile. He spoke quickly in Hebrew, explaining that he had a group of American college students visiting from the USA, who loved Israel and wanted to express their support to these soldiers. We were in the third week of the 2014 Gaza War, and missiles had been landing in southern Israel daily.

The soldiers looked skeptical and began to interrogate the pastor for the next five minutes. In typical Israeli fashion, there was much hand-motioning

---

[62] A Jewish seminary for women.

and excited dialogue. Finally the pastor turned and motioned for our team to get out of the cars. We walked slowly toward the fence bearing our gifts, smiling and greeting them with our "Shalom's" in thick Tennessee accents. Immediately the soldiers relaxed and radioed back to the operations building, and before we knew it, another ten soldiers had joined our merry band. We gave them the gifts we had brought, and were quite surprised to find that two of the soldiers were from The States, one from New York and the other from Los Angeles. It was quite common for American Jews to come and serve in the Israeli Defense Force (IDF). At least three of the troops were women. Most of them could speak conversational English, and we struck up friendly small-talk about their families and where they were from. At the end of the time together, I found myself in the middle of a group picture thinking:

This is surreal. I'm not in Kansas anymore.

As we walked back to the car, the Russian pastor announced that he would take a small group from our team further south to Ashkelon, barely thirteen miles away from Hamas' hostile missile launch sites on the Gaza Strip. Five of our young men volunteered to go, excited for the adventure. The rest of us headed back to Jerusalem for an evening Bible study with local believers. I prayed silently for Father God to protect our team as they went to visit another Iron Dome site in Ashkelon.

> "The wicked have laid a snare for me,
> but I do not stray from your precepts."
>
> Psalm 119:110 ESV

"Hi, you all," two of our team members introduced themselves to the IDF soldiers in Ashkelon, and soon found themselves deep in conversation about U.S.-Israeli relations. The team ended up spending almost two hours there and were given IDF t-shirts as souvenirs from the friendly soldiers. My son, Kanaan, was among the five, and asked the soldiers, "When do the missiles start falling? I heard that every evening, it's like fireworks exploding over the city."

"That's true," said the soldier. "It is strangely quiet tonight. Usually by this time, there are several dozen missiles that are shot down by our perimeter defense systems."

It was late that night when the team finally arrived back at our apartment, deep in the heart of Jerusalem. We said a prayer to the Lord, giving thanks that everyone was now back safely.

It was the next day, in Teddy Park, when we found out the rest of the story from the two Orthodox young women.

"Did you hear what happened yesterday evening down in Ashkelon?" they asked.

"No, tell us," Kendra, one of our team leaders, said.

"The Iron Dome missile system malfunctioned and was not operating for more than four hours. During that time, no missiles were shot out of Gaza into Israel," said one of the girls.

My face must have portrayed my shock, because the other girl said, "Why are you so surprised? The God of Israel was protecting us."

We ended up spending another hour in deep conversation with these girls, talking about our faith in the One True God and His Son, Jesus. I will never forget that night as long as I live, realizing that the hand of God was protecting not only our team, but my son as well, from the attack of the enemy.

Beloved, the God of Israel is the same yesterday, today, and forever.[63] The God who protected the citizens of Ashkelon and our five Caleb men that night back in 2014 is the same God who protects you and me today. Rest well tonight. Our security is not based upon the firepower of our nation, but rather the mighty right Hand of God. Selah.

Journal

Recall a time when you were in great danger, but the Hand of the Lord protected you. Write down your testimony in accordance with Revelation 12:11.[64] Share your testimony with three people this week.

Prayer

Abba, thank You that our security does not depend upon men but according to Your promises in the Word, that You will never leave us nor forsake us. Remind us that we do not live for this world, but for eternity to come.

In the Name of Jesus!

---

[63] Hebrews 13:8 NIV
[64] "They triumphed over him [satan] by the blood of the Lamb and by the word of their testimony."

Hebrew Treasure

Thomas L. Boehm

Nun נ

What do you need when you go into a dark room and cannot see? You need a source of light! A primary source of light is a lamp and the Hebrew word for lamp is nayr (נֵר). This stanza begins in verse 105 with this Hebrew word for lamp and the word begins with the letter nun (נ). Proverbs 6:23 also uses the Hebrew words for lamp and light to refer to the illuminating value of a good father's instructions. As a father of five children, I am very aware of my imperfections as a parent. I am grateful that our heavenly Father is perfect and His instructions as a good Father did not merely come in the form of written words but also in the form of a living Word — Messiah Jesus. He is the source of the Father's good instruction and offers illumination as the light of the world. Jesus called himself the "light of the world" (John 8:12; 9:5) and John calls the very life of Jesus the "light of men" (John 1:4). Not only does Jesus shine brightly in our ever darkening world, but as His followers, we shine His light as well. In fact, Proverbs 13:9 contrasts the shining light of the righteous with the snuffed out lamp (nayr) of the wicked. As those seeking to follow our Heavenly King while here on earth, let us meditate on Paul's words in 1 Corinthians 2:10-11, "The Spirit searches all things, even the deep things of God. For who knows a person's thoughts except their own spirit within them? In the same way no one knows the thoughts of God except the Spirit of God." Paul was likely illuminating and shining for us his reflections on Proverbs 20:27, "The spirit of man is the lamp (nayr) of the LORD, searching all his innermost parts." Let God's Spirit search you today, Beloved, and lead you by His illuminating light deeper into the Father's love and His good purposes for you!

Samekh - Worship with the Word - "Protector"
by Joseph Maloney

DAY 15

The Psalm 119 Journey

ס

Samekh

113 I hate the double-minded,
   but I love your law.

114 You are my hiding place and my shield;
   I hope in your word.

115 Depart from me, you evildoers,
   that I may keep the commandments of my God.

116 Uphold me according to your promise, that I may live,
   and let me not be put to shame in my hope!

117 Hold me up, that I may be safe
   and have regard for your statutes continually!

118 You spurn all who go astray from your statutes,
   for their cunning is in vain.

119 All the wicked of the earth you discard like dross,
   therefore I love your testimonies.

120 My flesh trembles for fear of you,
   and I am afraid of your judgments.

Knocking on Heaven's Floor
Though we stumble,
God's faithfulness will uphold us.

"How do you feel about jumping out of a plane today?" Adam, the skydiving videographer whom we had paid to chronicle our adventure, asked me.

"Excited," I replied. "The last time I jumped out of a perfectly good plane was fifteen years ago off the coast of southern Thailand."

Adam responded, "Are you nervous?"

"Yes!" I replied. "I've got a lot of adrenaline flowing through me right now," I said, beaming.

"Any last words that you want to share before you get on the plane?" Adam asked me.

"Follow God for the rest of your life," I declared with conviction.

It was September 10th, 2017, and my good buddy, Cody Weeks, and I were using a Groupon skydiving voucher. I had originally surprised my wife and one of her best friends with the voucher at the beginning of the summer. My wife made it known that there was no way they were going to jump out of a plane. When I called Cody and invited him on this adventure, he was all in.

We jumped into my car in Franklin, Tennessee, and headed down I-45 Southeast to Tullahoma, where Skydive Tennessee was located. After filling out liability waivers in triplicate and watching a safety video, we were outfitted with reinforced skydiving harnesses that we strapped on. The safety instructor checked our harnesses multiple times before we headed out to the tarmac where the PAC 750 single-engine plane stood majestically in the sunlight.

After some banter back and forth with Adam, he introduced me to Jackson, my jumpmaster, whom I would trust my life with for the next 45 minutes.

"Just so you know, when we get on the plane we will be sitting on the floor right next to the open fuselage door," Jackson informed me.

"Really!!" I exclaimed, my eyebrows rising and my stomach beginning to churn.

"No worries," he laughed. "I've done this hundreds of times and never lost anybody."

We crossed the tarmac slowly, as I pushed a walker that was assisting me. After three years with ALS, I wore boots with braces in them to support both my legs. One of the blessings I had received from this diagnosis was that now I lived every day as a gift.

Jackson put my back up against the edge of the plane and then with a hoist, lifted me onto the floorboard. Boarding and sitting down, he locked in four carabiners to the back of my harness. My back was now effectively superglued to his chest.

The plane began taxiing down the runway, building up speed to take off into the crisp fall afternoon. The roar of the engine filled the plane as I joked with Jackson, "When is the stewardess going to do the safety demonstration?"

Soon the white bird lifted off the ground and steadily rose into the vast sky. Within a few minutes, we were thousands of feet in the air, and the airfield below began to look like markings on a topographical map. Jackson yelled into my ear, "We'll be jumping within ten minutes!" as air blasted us from the door opening inches from my foot. It's surprising how many thoughts can go through your mind when you potentially face the end of your life. Skydiving is a calculated risk. You are hoping that there is a high probability that your jumpmaster is of sound mind and is planning a future for himself.

Thank you, Lord, for the gift of life, I spoke quietly in my heart. Thank You that You have given me many years in Your Kingdom and on the mission field. Thank You that You have allowed me to stand on the Great Wall of China, view the night skyline of Paris from the Eiffel Tower, and see with my own eyes the white-robed, colossal Mt. Everest. Thank You that You gave me opportunities to share Jesus with my Buddhist friends over street food in Bangkok, Thailand. Thank You for my beautiful, godly wife, Samantha, and my seven children. Thank You for breath in my lungs and a beating heart. Thank You that You have taught me to number my days, that I might gain a heart of wisdom.[65] Time stood still as I reflected with great gratitude on my life and the opportunities God had given me.

"It's time to roll, we're at 14,000 feet!" Jackson shouted as he maneuvered us to the open door, thrusting my legs out dangling into space. He reached up and grabbed a handrail and yelled, "1-2-3 JUMP!" We were hurled face-forward out into the sky as cold air pummeled our bodies, and a roar filled our ears as we free-fell.

I looked over to our right, and Adam was grinning ear-to-ear as he made a circular motion with his right finger. I looked at him, puzzled, as he had not informed me on the ground of what this hand signal meant. He flew toward us and put out his hand to give me a high-five. When I reached out, he grabbed my hand and spun us, causing us to rotate wildly like a top. The shock of the experience made my adrenaline spike. We finally leveled out, and after getting my bearings, I looked to the horizon, stunned by the beauty of the cobalt blue sky.

> "The heavens declare the glory of God; the skies proclaim the work of his hands."
>
> Psalm 19:1 NIV

This verse had become a favorite of mine on the mission field when hiking the hills of northern Thailand. There's nothing like a brilliant sky with no clouds to mark it. What a gift it is to see the work of the Master Creator, to

---

[65] Psalm 90:12 NIV

recognize that the Almighty God is the One who set the firmament in place.

We had been free-falling when suddenly, Jackson pulled the ripcord. Our rapid descent was arrested with a violent yank, and we shot upward. Floating down, stillness surrounded us, and I took in the rolling Tennessee countryside. What stunning beauty. I thanked God for our safety, not realizing that danger lurked below.

We were now under 1,000 feet, and I began to review the landing in my mind.

"If you extend your legs straight out as we land, I will take the brunt of the impact," Jackson had told me during our jump rehearsal an hour before. "If you can't, don't worry. I will make sure everything works out."

I wondered to myself, How is this going to turn out exactly? As the ground rushed up at us, I tried to lift my legs and realized that the combination of gravity and ALS was keeping them down.

WHAM…we slammed into the grass field, and my legs buckled beneath me. I bit my lip as the pain made me think I had broken them. A female assistant ran up, grabbed my ankles, and straightened out my legs. "Are you alright?" she asked me. I tried to act cavalier and mask the throbbing in my thigh muscles. My walker was ready for me, and I started limping across the field, being interviewed by Adam.

"Would you do it again?" Adam laughingly asked me.

"Absolutely," I breathlessly exclaimed.

Life is a gift from God, and I want to live it to the fullest.

> "Hold me up, that I may be safe
> and have regard for your statutes continually!"

Psalm 119:117 ESV

Beloved, is it possible that skydiving is part of God's Kingdom? To some, it might not seem spiritual, but to understand God's Kingdom, we must understand God's ways. Religion would seek to compartmentalize our lives and separate the spiritual from the natural. In His Kingdom, He reigns and rules over all. To the man and woman of God, it all belongs to Him. Our lives are not our own; they belong to Him. Nature is a gift to mankind from the very heart of the Father. I feel closest to Him in His creation, in total awe of the beauty that He has made.

Free-falling on that September day five years ago, I was in awe of the sky that stretched out across the horizon as far as I could see. I had been in the trenches battling ALS, and this was a welcomed adventure experiencing the presence of God.

When I came in for the landing and my legs buckled underneath me, it was a painful experience, but even in that trial, God was with me. I am grateful for His grace that protected my legs from being broken. I have thought many times over the years of the fact that God has watched over me and has faithfully kept me from many calamities. The writer of Proverbs penned these words:

"For though a righteous man falls seven times, he rises again."

Proverbs 24:16a NIV 1984

Selah.

Journal

How have you experienced God through His creation?

Where on earth do you encounter God the most?

Recount God's faithfulness in sparing you from tragedy.

*Follow the QR code to watch Steve's skydiving adventure!

Prayer

Abba, Father, thank You that You have kept my feet from stumbling, my legs from failing, and have watched over my path. You are the Faithful One. You deserve all adoration, praise, and worship. May my daily life reflect this reality. With great love and honor.

In the Name of Jesus!

Hebrew Treasure
Thomas L. Boehm

Samekh ס

Read verses 114 and 120 again. Consider the way the protection and hope described in verse 114 is contrasted with the trembling and fear in verse 120. There seems to be a contradiction between the safety David describes in the first case and the dread he describes in the second. But the fear David describes in verse 120 is the fear of the LORD. In the book of Exodus, Moses describes the fear of the LORD as having the protective purpose "to keep you from sinning" (Ex. 20:20). God had actually informed Moses beforehand that the visitation on Mt. Sinai in fire and smoke and trumpet blasts would be for the expressed purpose of driving people's trust toward Moses as God's authorized messenger (Ex. 19:9) and that this was good (see Deut. 4:10, 36; 5:5, 28–29). Proverbs 1:7 and 9:10 further explain the fear of the LORD as the pathway into the protection and presence of God. The Hebrew word sit'ri (סִתְרִי) opens verse 114, begins with the letter samekh (ס), and comes from the root word meaning "hiding place." God is David's hiding place and his shield. Psalm 27:5 uses the same Hebrew word for hiding place to describe God's tent or tabernacle. Furthermore, Psalm 31:20 uses the same word to describe his hiding place as the very presence of God Himself. Fear and trembling can actually be good if in response to the presence and holiness of God Who alone can satisfy our thirsty souls. God alone is a trustworthy and protective hiding place where true true safety can be found. Run to Him in prayer, abide in Him through faith, and rest in Him as your hiding place!

Ayin - Worship With The Word - "Pledge of Good"
by Mark Woodward

DAY 16

The Psalm 119 Journey

ע

Ayin

121 I have done what is just and right;
   do not leave me to my oppressors.

122 Give your servant a pledge of good;
   let not the insolent oppress me.

123 My eyes long for your salvation
   and for the fulfillment of your righteous promise.

124 Deal with your servant according to your steadfast love,
   and teach me your statutes.

125 I am your servant; give me understanding,
   that I may know your testimonies!

126 It is time for the Lord to act,
   for your law has been broken.

127 Therefore I love your commandments
   above gold, above fine gold.

128 Therefore I consider all your precepts to be right;
   I hate every false way.

The Old City
Man cannot create peace.
It can only come through the Prince of Peace.

"These ceramic bowls are hand-painted by Arab artisans in the city of Hebron," the friendly shopkeeper shared with me. It was the day before we were to return to the United States; I was in the Old City of Jerusalem, in the Arab Christian section where shops lined the ancient cobblestone alleyways. It was July of 2014, and I was helping to lead a team of college students with Caleb Company. We had spent a full month traveling the length and width of Israel visiting Messianic believers, seeing the ancient Biblical sites, and serving at a retreat center in the desert of Kadesh Barnea on the Egyptian border.

"You must be from America," the shopkeeper stated as he smiled at me.

"Yes I am," I said. "How has business been for you this past month?"

His face fell as he slowly responded, "Not good, not good my friend. The conflict between Gaza and Israel has caused all the tourists to leave. Without tourists, I have very little business, and it's difficult to feed my family." Before I knew it, the shopkeeper had invited me to sit down and poured some mint tea.

"This conflict between Jew and Arab has been here for thousands of years, has it not?" I asked him.

"Yes, the sons of Jacob and the sons of Ishmael have been in contention for many millennia.[66] My family has been in this land for many generations, but

---

[66] Associated Press. "Israeli Police Storm Jerusalem Holy Site After Rock-Throwing." NPR, NPR, 22 Apr. 2022, www.npr.org/2022/04/22/1094237785/israeli-police-storm-jerusalem-holy-site-

the last few decades have seen a rise in the fighting between our two peoples. I am a Christian and believe in Jesus, the Son of God."

I smiled and responded, "I am too; we are brothers in the family of God." We spent another twenty minutes talking about our families, culture, and the present conflict in the Middle East. The very last words he shared had a deep impact on me:

"The only way that peace will come to the Middle East is through the Prince of Peace," he said with deep emotion. We ended in prayer and I left his store carrying several bags of ceramic gifts.

Beloved, are you standing on the truth of God's promises for Israel?[67] No politician, ambassador, or government has ever been able to solve the conflict in the Middle East. We as the Ecclesia, the people of God, have an opportunity and a responsibility to intercede for Israel, to stand as watchmen on the walls.[68] King David wrote these words in Psalm 119:

---

after-rock-throwing.

[67] Then I saw "a new heaven and a new earth," for the first heaven and the first earth had passed away, and there was no longer any sea. I saw the Holy City, the new Jerusalem, coming down out of heaven from God, prepared as a bride beautifully dressed for her husband. And I heard a loud voice from the throne saying, "Look! God's dwelling place is now among the people, and he will dwell with them. They will be his people, and God himself will be with them and be their God. 'He will wipe every tear from their eyes. There will be no more death' or mourning or crying or pain, for the old order of things has passed away." He who was seated on the throne said, "I am making everything new!" Then he said, "Write this down, for these words are trustworthy and true." He said to me: "It is done. I am the Alpha and the Omega, the Beginning and the End. To the thirsty I will give water without cost from the spring of the water of life. Those who are victorious will inherit all this, and I will be their God and they will be my children." Revelation 21:1-7 NIV

[68] I have posted watchmen on your walls, Jerusalem;
they will never be silent day or night.
You who call on the Lord,
give yourselves no rest,
and give him no rest till he establishes Jerusalem

> "My eyes long for your salvation
>
> and for the fulfillment of your righteous promise."
>
> Psalm 119:123 ESV

As we steward the promises of God, we pray through until the breakthrough.[69] Peace in the Middle East will only be achieved when the Son of Man returns. God is faithful. He will fulfill His Word. He is a covenant-keeping God, and He will keep His Word to Israel, as well as to the sons of Ishmael. Our prayers as believing Gentiles are a key to Jewish eyes being opened.[70] With the opening of their eyes, they will see Yeshua high and lifted up, and they will usher in His return.[71] Beloved, may we be faithful in this prayer.

Journal

Read Romans chapters 9, 10, and 11. What does Paul say to us Gentiles about the importance of Israel in these last days?

How are you standing with Israel to see the blood family of Jesus restored

---

and makes her the praise of the earth.
Isaiah 62:6-7 NIV

[69] For no matter how many promises God has made, they are "Yes" in Christ. And so through him the "Amen" is spoken by us to the glory of God. II Corinthians 1:20 NIV

[70] Again I ask: Did they stumble so as to fall beyond recovery? Not at all! Rather, because of their transgression, salvation has come to the Gentiles to make Israel envious. But if their transgression means riches for the world, and their loss means riches for the Gentiles, how much greater riches will their full inclusion bring! Romans 11:11-12 NIV

[71] For I tell you, you will not see me again until you say, "Blessed is he who comes in the name of the Lord." Matthew 23:39 NIV

to the Kingdom of God?

Prayer

Father God, thank You that You have called me to be a watchman for Israel, to stand on her walls in the Spirit and cry out for her eyes to be opened, that she would turn to Jesus her Messiah and receive Him as King. Thank You for the sacrifice of Jewish apostles two thousand years ago, who brought the gospel to us, the Gentile nations, and gave their lives on our behalf. May I be willing to give my life on their behalf to see them return to You.

In the Name of Jesus!

Hebrew Treasure

Thomas L. Boehm

Ayin ע

"Death before disobedience" is the cry of the underground church in many parts of the world. This declaration reflects deep allegiance and marks a true disciple and follower of Jesus. But this is a high bar. We often fall short. Which is why the unending mercies of God are so precious in the cleansing blood of Jesus (1 Jo. 1:9). This declaration of allegiance and servanthood to the extreme degree should provoke us to deeper surrender to following Jesus as his blood-bought servant. Beginning with the Hebrew letter ayin, the Hebrew word for servant is eved and is the first word of verse 125. Specifically, verse 125 begins Av-d'cha (עַבְדְּךָ) which begins with the letter ayin (ע) and means Your servant. David is declaring himself to be God's servant. After committing their lives to serve Jesus, the Jewish disciples Paul (Rom. 1:1; Phil. 1:1; Tit. 1:1), James (1:1), Peter (2 Pet. 1:1), and Jude (1:1) often started their letters by affirming their primary identity as a slave or servant (eved) and declaring their allegiance to Jesus. John also addresses the last book of the Bible to you and me as slaves of Jesus for the sake of making Him known (Rev. 1:1). Peter goes on to defend the ultimate freedom available in serving Jesus over everything and everyone by declaring "a man is a slave to whatever has mastered him" (2 Pe. 2:19). Beloved, Jesus has mastered and overcome death and slavery to him is the greatest path of true freedom. "Don't you know that when you offer yourselves to someone as obedient slaves, you are slaves of the one you obey — whether you are slaves to sin, which leads to death, or to obedience, which leads to righteousness?" (Rom. 6:16).

Pe - Worship with the Word - "Your Testimonies Are Wonderful" by Joseph Maloney

DAY 17
The Psalm 119 Journey

פ

Pe

129 Your testimonies are wonderful;
   therefore my soul keeps them.

130 The unfolding of your words gives light;
   it imparts understanding to the simple.

131 I open my mouth and pant,
   because I long for your commandments.

132 Turn to me and be gracious to me,
   as is your way with those who love your name.

133 Keep steady my steps according to your promise,
   and let no iniquity get dominion over me.

134 Redeem me from man's oppression,
   that I may keep your precepts.

135 Make your face shine upon your servant,
   and teach me your statutes.

136 My eyes shed streams of tears,
   because people do not keep your law.

North Korea

Those who truly live
Are those who have learned to die.

"There is no other name under Heaven by which men can be saved." My father, Sid Allen, declared these words in Korean. The year was 1972 and my father, a missionary to South Korea, along with my Uncle Rand, had been invited to a Republic of Korea Army base around six miles from the DMZ[72] border that separated communist North Korea from South Korea. The soldiers, 120 strong, sat cross-legged in rows, listening intently as my father shared the simple gospel.

"Your dad was the real deal, Steve," my uncle's voice broke as he spoke. "Your father spoke to those soldiers about men being under authority.[73] He told them that the greatest leaders were those who had learned to serve like Jesus." My uncle went on, "Your father did not speak long, maybe 7-10 minutes. But at the end he gave a clear invitation to receive Jesus as Lord. Hands shot up and many prayed the sinner's prayer. I was twenty years old at the time, and as I looked out over the sea of men, I realized that we were around the same age. I was already a believer but was impacted by both the humility and authority that your father walked in. He never called attention to himself but always pointed others to Jesus."

Some of my favorite memories from growing up in Korea were going to the farm near the DMZ border with my dad. He was a medical missionary, and as a veterinarian, he was taking care of over 100 dairy cows that were used to produce milk that contained Vitamin D for combating tuberculosis, a

---

[72] The Demilitarized Zone (DMZ) is a region on the Korean peninsula that demarcates North Korea from South Korea. Roughly following the 38th parallel, the 150-mile-long DMZ incorporates territory on both sides of the cease-fire line as it existed at the end of the Korean War (1950–53).
History.com Editors. "Demilitarized Zone." History.com, A&E Television Networks, 14 June 2010, https://www.history.com/topics/korea/demilitarized-zone#:~:text=The%20Demilitarized%20Zone%20(DMZ)%20is,War%20(1950%E2%80%9353).
[73] Matthew 8:5-13

rampant malady in South Korea. I enjoyed hearing stories from his childhood on the truck ride up from Seoul, the capital, to the farm. I would walk closely behind him as he made his rounds through the barn, examining and treating the cows. Lunch would be peanut butter sandwiches that my mother would wrap in wax paper, and a large thermos of Campbell's™ alphabet soup. For a six-year-old, this was big stuff. It didn't get any better than this.

Years later, in talking to family members, they shared my father's heart for North Korea, that he would often stop and pray when he was at the farm, looking north to the hills across the DMZ, where the communist country lay shrouded in mystery. He ended up traveling to North Korea five times as a consultant to a goat farm initiative that was run by a European NGO.[74]

In 2003, my father traveled to Mongolia with an Australian missionary to investigate the possibility of purchasing a specialized black goat that would help strengthen the genetics of the North Korean herds. The trip turned out to be quite the adventure as they found themselves bumping down potholed roads in the middle of a blizzard. They were in a large van with an assortment of Mongolian and Korean passengers, as well as a translator-guide. My father was looking for the governor of a province that was his contact for possibly purchasing a number of the goats to take back into North Korea.

"Uh oh," the Australian missionary exclaimed. "I think we're out on a lake." The blizzard had effectively whitewashed everything around them, and unknowingly the Mongolian driver had driven out onto the frozen surface. When he realized where they were, he quickly made a U-turn and returned back safely to the land. There was a great sense of collective relief when the passengers comprehended that they had just averted disaster. It was only an hour later that the van ground to a halt in the middle of a country road, high-centered on a dirt mound that had been covered by the snow. The driver frantically shifted between forward and reverse to free the van, but to no avail. They were now stranded in a remote corner of Mongolia.

---

[74] NGO - "Non-governmental Organization"

Several hours and not a few passionate prayers later, a farm truck appeared and in a matter of minutes had winched them free from their prison. It was just before dawn when they arrived at a small town guest house. After a few hours of sleep, they found they were not the only guests, as they scratched a number of bug bites.

Following a number of inquiries, their guide informed them that the governor was nearby and ready to meet. Later that day, after conferring with the governor and making a few phone calls, my father determined it would be best to take frozen goat embryos back to North Korea. Artificial insemination into the herd was better than transporting live goats, as the governor informed him that the North Korean guards would not allow animals to cross the border.

Toward the end of my father's life he developed Parkinson's Disease. He and my mother had moved to a retirement community in Nashville, Tennessee. Two years before passing, he asked our family that his ashes be scattered in North Korea. At the time we had no idea how we would accomplish it, but simply gave it to the Lord in prayer. Later, John Lee[75] and his wife, who had worked at the goat farm as part of the NGO management, flew back from North Korea to speak at my father's memorial and agreed to take some of my father's ashes back. On November 17th, 2018, to mark my father's birthday, John scattered my father's ashes under an oak tree that overlooked the sloping hills of the goat farm. My father's last wishes were honored, and his body now lay at rest on the sacred soil of the nation that has been most resistant to the gospel.

Beloved, my father was quiet and humble. He did not seek attention or the praise of man. His greatness came from his continual service to those around him. Great leaders have learned to serve. My father's legacy will be marked in eternity because he gave his life to proclaiming the gospel on the Korean Peninsula. In word and deed, he preached Jesus. The Lord honored him by numbering his days and watching over his steps. King David spoke of this

---

[75] Not his real name.

faithfulness in Psalm 119:

> "Keep steady my steps according to your promise,
> and let no iniquity get dominion over me."

Psalm 119:133 ESV

The man of God, who knows the Father, does not fear the future, for he knows the future is in the Father's hands. When we truly know God, we trust Him, and when We trust Him, we are able to do great exploits in His Name. Our lives were not meant for this earth, but rather for the Kingdom to come. When we truly know His promises, our lives will be a reflection of the faithfulness of God. We are to be signposts that point those in the darkness to the light. Selah.

Journal

What made Jesus such a great leader?

If the greatest in the Kingdom is a servant-leader, how are you growing in this role?

Name three people that you admire who are true servant-leaders. What do you admire about them?

Prayer

Abba Father, thank You that You sent Your Son, Jesus, to show us the way of greatness, to model for us what servant-leadership is. Thank You that in everything that you have called us to do, You have empowered us to do it. May I spend my life in this pursuit, to be the hands and feet of Jesus to all those around me, to show the world the greatest love of all, the love of Jesus.

In the Name of Jesus!

Hebrew Treasure
Thomas L. Boehm

Pe פ

God told Moses how He wanted to bless His people in Numbers 6:22-27. There at Mt. Sinai, God gave specific instructions for Moses to pass on to God's priestly representatives on earth to literally put God's Name on them and bless them (v. 27). Part of this familiar priestly blessing is for God to "shine His face upon you" (v. 25) and "turn His face toward you" (v. 26). That's a lot of talk about God's face. Apparently, He wanted His face on our lips as those called to be a priesthood of believers to bless others. You might even say God wanted His face in our face (cf. Gen. 32:30; Ex. 33:11; Num. 14:14; Deut. 5:4)! The way to say Your face in Hebrew is Pa'neh'cha (פָּנֶיךָ) and is the first word in Psalm 119:135, beginning with the letter pe (פ). God's face shining on His servant (servant in Hebrew is eved; see previous stanza), in this verse, is connected to Spirit-led instruction of God's statutes. This is parallel to the illumination described in verse 130, "The unfolding of your words gives light; it imparts understanding to the simple." I am so grateful that God's face has been revealed in Jesus. John, therefore, reminds us of the words of Jesus who declared, "Anyone who has seen me has seen the Father" (Jn. 14:9). When you are in distress, try praying that God would restore you by shining His face upon you like Asaph did in Psalm 80:3, 7, and 19. Remember, God wants us to abide in His countenance (Jn. 15) and Jesus will never let us down.

Tsadhe - Worship with the Word - "Zeal"
by Joseph Maloney

DAY 18
The Psalm 119 Journey

צ

Tsadhe

137 Righteous are you, O Lord,
   and right are your rules.

138 You have appointed your testimonies in righteousness
   and in all faithfulness.

139 My zeal consumes me,
   because my foes forget your words.

140 Your promise is well tried,
   and your servant loves it.

141 I am small and despised,
   yet I do not forget your precepts.

142 Your righteousness is righteous forever,
   and your law is true.

143 Trouble and anguish have found me out,
   but your commandments are my delight.

144 Your testimonies are righteous forever;
   give me understanding that I may live.

Five Words
When we freely serve the poor,
We are intentionally serving Jesus.

"We are not in Kansas anymore," said Lawrence, one of my teammates, as we looked out the window of the rickety bus. We were riding from the airport to our hotel in downtown Calcutta, India. Thirty minutes into our drive, one of the rear tires blew out. I was expecting us to pull over to repair it, but instead we kept driving. I'm not sure why we didn't stop, but evidently the bus driver was not eager to spend any time in this part of town. We were in one of the poorest cities on earth, and all around, poverty glared back at us. It was dusk, and as we clanked through the congested streets, the bus shook because of the blown tire. City blocks were cast into darkness as the electricity failed. We were being introduced to "brown-outs," rolling outages when sections of the city would lose power for a few hours before coming back on.

A recent 1988 college graduate, I was on a three-month mission trip around the world with fifteen young people, our mentor, Stanley Shipp, and his wife, Marie. It was an amazing experience studying cultures, sitting at the feet of missionaries, and encountering the lost.

Our plane ride from Bangkok to Calcutta earlier that afternoon was daunting to say the least. We boarded our Indian Airlines flight on time but recognized that there were no attendants on the plane yet. When the pilot boarded, we noticed that his shirt was unbuttoned to mid-chest and stained with coffee. Several of our teammates looked at each other with raised eyebrows. Soon a steward and a stewardess boarded for this regional flight. At the last minute, ten Indian teenagers got on the flight, all with identical jeans, jean jackets, and leather briefcases. An older man was the evident ringleader, and after overhearing some conversation from passengers, we realized that this was a black market gang carrying clothes, electronics, and liquor that they would resell for a sizable profit in India. The steward ended up getting into a heated argument with the ringleader and in a fit of anger pounded on the closed cabin door, yelling for the ground crew to open up. To our astonishment and angst, the steward exited and never reappeared.

After a three-hour flight, we landed on the tarmac in Calcutta. There was only one other airplane parked nearby, a Russian Aeroflot commercial plane. The black market gang aggressively pushed to the front and disembarked first, striding toward Immigration with the rest of us following them. We entered the dingy building with an old sign out front that said "Arrival Hall" in three languages. In what appeared to be a well-rehearsed occurrence, the ringleader of the gang walked to the front of the line, opened his briefcase, and set two bottles of whiskey on the counter. The official took the two bottles and briskly waved them through.

I had much to think about on the bus ride to our hotel after that disturbing experience. We take a lot for granted in our sterile first-world bubbles. In the Third World, life can be cheap, and a worldview of fatalism is the course for the day. By the time we reached the hotel, I was running a slight fever after developing a sinus infection in Bangkok. The next morning, I stayed back at the hotel to rest while our team left for a tour of the city.

It was late afternoon when Brad and Lawrence, two of my college buddies and best friends, walked in the door. "You missed it, Steve!" Brad exclaimed. "We met Mother Teresa this morning at the Missionaries of Charity clinic.[76] We were told she was not in town, but evidently she flew in late last night after we arrived."

"I can't believe it!" I moaned as I looked up at the ceiling, realizing that I had missed a once-in-a-lifetime opportunity.

Lawrence shared their encounter from that morning:

---

[76] In the words of Mother Teresa, the Missionaries of Charity would care for "the hungry, the naked, the homeless, the crippled, the blind, the lepers, all those people who feel unwanted, unloved, uncared for throughout society, people that have become a burden to the society and are shunned by everyone" ("washingtonpost.com: Highlights of Mother Teresa's Life". www.washingtonpost.com. Archived from the original on 1 January 2018. Retrieved 14 April 2022.)

"She held up her right hand and then said 'Five words.'" She stood not more than four feet ten inches, wearing a white veil, her face leathery and brown after years of being in the tropic heat.

'You did it unto me,' Mother Teresa continued as she recounted the words of Jesus.[77] When we help the poorest of the poor, we are ministering to Jesus. It is our privilege and honor."

Lawrence went on with the story, "Our team took out their cameras and started taking pictures. With ferocity, Mother Teresa pointed her finger at us, saying, 'You should sell your cameras and give the money to the poor.' The room fell silent as there was not much to say in response to the convicting words of this living saint."

Years later, this story from our world tour mission trip became one of the most remembered and retold.

Beloved, the Word of God instructs us to help the poor, the marginalized, and the homeless.[78] On the Final Day, we will be judged according to how we treated the poor in our midst. Mother Teresa and her Sisters of Mercy quietly served the destitute and dying of Calcutta for decades.

Read the words of King David in this verse below:

> "You have appointed your testimonies in righteousness
> and in all faithfulness."
>
> Psalm 119:138 ESV

Mother Teresa became a living testimony of the righteousness of God in the midst of a fallen world. We are not saved by our works, but our works

---

[77] Matthew 25:34-40

[78] "Religion that God our Father accepts as pure and faultless is this: to look after orphans and widows in their distress and to keep oneself from being polluted by the world." James 1:27 NIV

are in response to the amazing grace of God, freely given to us. He appointed these works to us before the beginning of time.[79] When we partner with the Lord in serving the poor around us, we become living testimonies. Selah.

Journal

Recall a time this past year when you served the poor and shared with the lost.

How can you grow as a living testimony of righteousness in your community?

How can these works, appointed to us before the beginning of time, be a gift and not a burden in the light of the grace of God?

Prayer

Abba Father, thank You that daily You are growing me in my identity as a child of God, and in this identity, I am learning to serve the poor around me. Thank You that You have appointed me to be a testimony of righteousness and faithfulness. It is Christ in me that makes this a reality.

In the Name of Jesus!

Hebrew Treasure
Thomas L. Boehm

Tsadhe צ

"Rules without relationship can lead to rebellion." This simple statement landed heavily on my heart as a new parent trying to raise godly children. I wanted to protect and guide my children but rules were not enough. To be

---

[79] "For we are God's handiwork, created in Christ Jesus to do good works, which God prepared in advance for us to do." Ephesians 2:10 NIV

fruitful, rules must function within the context of foundationally healthy and loving relationships. Accordingly, Psalm 119:137 identifies God's rules as good and right but the second half of the verse identifies the very quality of "rightness," or righteousness, as being the very essence and character of God Himself. Thus, verse 137 begins with the Hebrew word for righteous, Tsa'deek (צַדִּיק), beginning with the letter tsadhe (צ). David uses the noun form of this word four more times in this stanza. Verses 138 and 144 use righteousness to describe God's testimonies. Verse 142 uses this word twice to identify the everlasting nature of God and His righteousness beginning with three Hebrew words translated, "Your righteousness" — "is righteous" — "forever" (l'olam, see chapter 12 Hebrew Treasure), and ending with two Hebrew words translated, "your law" (torah, instruction) "is truth." While we tend to focus on our "doing" right things and obeying right rules, there is a deeper "rightness" connected to God's very being rather than merely our doing. What we do certainly matters, but what God has done, is doing, and will do, matters more. He is the true source of our righteousness. As Paul says in Romans 3:21, "But now apart from the law the righteousness of God has been made known, to which the Law and the Prophets testify." Prioritize your relationship with God and He will protect and guide you as a perfect and righteous Father who knows you best and loves you most!

Qoph - Worship with the Word - "Nightwatch Knight"
by Joseph Maloney

DAY 19

The Psalm 119 Journey

ק

Qoph

145 With my whole heart I cry; answer me, O Lord!
   I will keep your statutes.

146 I call to you; save me,
   that I may observe your testimonies.

147 I rise before dawn and cry for help;
   I hope in your words.

148 My eyes are awake before the watches of the night,
   that I may meditate on your promise.

149 Hear my voice according to your steadfast love;
   O Lord, according to your justice give me life.

150 They draw near who persecute me with evil purpose;
   they are far from your law.

151 But you are near, O Lord,
   and all your commandments are true.

152 Long have I known from your testimonies
   that you have founded them forever.

The Nightwatch
Joseph Maloney
Many people meditate on God's Word during the day,
But the breakthrough often comes when we meditate on it during the night.[80]

We walked down Holly Avenue in East Nashville holding hands, shocked at the damage caused by the tornado that swept through on March 3rd, 2020. We arrived at my friend Andrew's house and I introduced him to my fiancée, Sherry. He was clearly exhausted, processing this traumatic event and we didn't know what to say to bring comfort to the situation. I had given Sherry a balloon earlier with a unicorn on it that said "Believe in unicorns." In a moment of childlike brilliance, she took a sharpie marker, crossed out the word "unicorns" and wrote "Jesus" making it say "Believe in Jesus." She gave it to Andrew and he broke into a gut-wrenching laugh which I could see brought relief and refreshment to his soul. It was a hilarious and beautiful moment in the midst of such devastating circumstances.

After waving goodbye, I took Sherry to the airport to fly back to Canada, and that was the last time I saw her…at least in person. Two weeks later the borders between the United States and Canada closed due to COVID-19, so we couldn't see each other. Four months later, she unexpectedly ended our relationship, sending me into a tailspin. Sometimes we learn about the nightwatch during the dark night of the soul seasons.

Qoph, the 19th letter of the Hebrew alphabet, has one key theme – the nightwatch is powerful! Psalm 119 is loaded with Davidic secrets; it is like getting a glimpse into King David's personal prayer notebook where he shares how he intimately connected with God. The best way to get a clear picture of someone's heart is to hear them pray. David was the man after God's own heart, so who better to shape our prayer life after? He understood that the most important aspect of our lives is our prayer life and that the most

---
[80] Joshua 1:8 ESV, Psalm 1:2 ESV

important legacy to leave is that of prayer. I believe that David's prayers directly affected Jesus' life, his future descendent.

So what is the nightwatch and why is it important? First of all, it can be broken down into four different watches that each last three hours and have a unique purpose.

- First Watch (6-9 p.m.) Reflection & Remembrance
- Second Watch (9-12 a.m.) Thanksgiving & Worship
- Third Watch (12-3 a.m.) Warfare & Breakthrough
- Fourth Watch (3-6 a.m.) Revelation & Consecration[81]

I want to specifically focus on the Fourth Watch because that is where God met me. After the break-up I went home to my parents' apple orchard in Northern California and spent a month getting back on my feet. God would wake me up around 3am and since I couldn't go back to sleep, I would walk around the apple orchard reciting Psalm 119 with the moon shining over me like a hopeful lantern.

Praying at night is different from praying during the day. Psalm 19:2 says, "Day to day pours out speech and night to night reveals knowledge." We receive knowledge from the Holy Spirit during the nighttime because there is a thin veil between the physical and spiritual realms, especially during the Fourth Watch. This is also when the most witchcraft and evil takes place. Knowledge causes our prayers to be more precise and effective, like an arrow hitting the bullseye. The Fourth Watch is a time to receive revelation of God's character and His ways but also revelation of spiritual barriers and how to overcome them. This watch is also a time of consecration, covering, and canceling of the enemy's assignments. Consecrating the day to the Lord looks like us prophesying the Word of God over it and declaring that His purposes

---

[81] https://www.abbaheart.com/prayer-watches

will prevail. Then I specifically pray a covering for my family members by pleading the blood of Jesus over them and asking God to remove every assignment of the enemy over their lives. The battle is always won in the place of prayer.

The devil wanted to drown me in a pool of hopelessness through the broken engagement. Thankfully, the Lord started to restore my soul during the Fourth Watch. God told me to go on a honeymoon with Jesus! So I road tripped across the USA, stopping in Idaho, Yellowstone, the Crow Reservation in Montana, Mount Rushmore, Chicago, and finally back to Nashville.

When I arrived back in Nashville, my two friends, Claude and Elias, came over to pray and fast for a week in my prayer room, which we called the Upper Room. The first thing they did was wash my feet; then they prayed and prophesied over me and my future wife. This filled me with hope and began a season of doing regular nightwatches with these two mighty men of God. Both African refugees, Claude and Elias had passion and dedication to prayer like no one else I knew. Even though they were about 10 years younger than me, I had a strong sense that I needed to be running with them because they had something that I wanted and they knew an aspect of prayer that I had not known, Warfare Intercession.

God nursed me back to life during that season as He taught me about the nightwatch, a deeper kind of prayer that dispatches angels, moves heaven, and brings tangible breakthrough.

Journal

What are the three areas of your life where you need the biggest breakthroughs?

What are some barriers that are keeping you from each of these promises?

Are you hungry enough for the promise that you will commit to one 3-hour nightwatch this week?

If so, when? _____ Whom will you do it with? _____

Signature: _____ Date: _____

*By signing this, you are making a commitment to do one watch this week.

Prayer

Gracious God, Heavenly Father, thank You that You are opening up my spiritual eyes to the power and significance of the nightwatch. Lord, I receive the seed of faith for the nightwatch and I desire for You to take me deeper in understanding the spirit of prayer, revelation, breakthrough, and knowledge that are uncovered during the night. Lord, Increase the capacity in my heart to store, understand, and utilize Your word as a sharp and dangerous sword against the enemy during the nightwatch. I pray this all in the mighty and life-giving name of Jesus Christ. Hallelujah!

In the Name of Jesus!

Hebrew Treasure

Thomas L. Boehm

Qoph ק

Have you ever called out to God for help? Desperate need can produce a desperate cry, or a calling out, for help. The Hebrew verb to call is qara and begins with the letter qoph. The first two verses in this stanza begin with a form of this verb depicting David's calling out to God for help. Specifically, verse 145 starts with the word Qa'ra'ti (קָרָאתִי) that begins with the Hebrew letter qoph (ק). David is crying out with his whole heart to God. Similarly, verse 146 starts with David crying out for help and for strength to obey God's good rules (i.e., testimonies, see chapter 18 Hebrew Treasure). David uses the same word in Psalm 130:1, "Out of the depths I cry to you, O LORD." But desperation is not the only motivator for calling or crying out. This word also reflects a deep desire for relationship. After God finishes creating the world and ordering all that is in it, the serpent strikes to bring disorder and division. In Genesis chapter 3, after deception and disobedience enter God's good creation, God calls to Adam (v. 9). Can you sense God's desire to rescue and restore the holy intimacy between God and His very good, but now fallen, humans? The first Hebrew word in Leviticus 1:1 begins with a form of qara, specifically, va'yiqra, meaning And God called. In the last chapter of Exodus, God had come down from Mt. Sinai and literally filled the newly built Tabernacle with His holy Presence (Ex. 40:34-35). Then, the very next verse opening the book of Leviticus starts with a connective conjunction "and" connected to a form of the word qara. This first word in Leviticus 1:1, va'yikra (And He called) describes God calling out to Moses whom God chose to be the authorized and delegated mediator to restore God's people to Himself. God desires relationship with His people. "Today, if you hear His voice, do not harden your hearts" (Ps. 95:1) but respond to His voice as He calls to you out of His desire to be with you and to lead you as He proves Himself capable of meeting your desperate need in Jesus!

Resh - Worship with the Word - "Song of the Afflicted"
by Joseph Maloney

DAY 20
The Psalm 119 Journey

ר

Resh

153 Look on my affliction and deliver me,
   for I do not forget your law.

154 Plead my cause and redeem me;
   give me life according to your promise!

155 Salvation is far from the wicked,
   for they do not seek your statutes.

156 Great is your mercy, O Lord;
   give me life according to your rules.

157 Many are my persecutors and my adversaries,
   but I do not swerve from your testimonies.

158 I look at the faithless with disgust,
   because they do not keep your commands.

159 Consider how I love your precepts!
   Give me life according to your steadfast love.

160 The sum of your word is truth,
   and every one of your righteous rules endures forever.

Life Lesson
When temptation knocks at the door,
Don't answer it.

"Steve, I've got a deal for you that you can't refuse!"

My buddy, Garth,[82] stood in the doorway of my freshman dorm room with a big smile on his face. Garth personified "big." He was a Texan, and everything about him was big: 6'3", big frame, big muscles, and big cowboy boots that he wore all the time.

"I'm heading down to the Mexican border this weekend, and I've got a contact on the other side who works in currency exchange. He said he can double our money if we don't delay. I'll even guarantee your investment since you're a Bible major."

As a college student, I didn't have a lot of money, but I thought to myself, "Wow, what an easy way to make a quick buck."

"Do you take checks?" I asked Garth.

"No pro-blem-o!" Garth cracked.

I quickly wrote out a check for $200 from my meager bank account and handed him my humble contribution. Garth folded the check and with a big grin, disappeared down the hall. The weekend sped by, and Monday morning I saw Garth walking across the lawn in front of the school cafeteria, appropriately called "The Bean."

I yelled out, "Garth! How did it go?"

The first indicator that things were not right was that the big smile that normally plastered Garth's face had disappeared. Dark circles were under his eyes, and I could tell that he was not in a good mood.

---

[82] Not his real name, to protect his identity.

"Uh…" Garth looked at the ground and kicked the lawn. "It didn't turn out like I thought it would. I lost all the money." He looked me straight in the eye. "But I am a man of my word, and here is your money back." He handed me $200 in cash.

"Thanks," I stammered, surprised that I had escaped the guillotine. "Sorry that it didn't work out," I muttered.

As I walked away from Garth, the Holy Spirit quietly spoke in my heart, "Greed is not a worthy companion, son. He always takes more than you bargain for."

> "Great is your mercy, O Lord;
> give me life according to your rules."
>
> Psalm 119:156 ESV

Beloved, why is our flesh so predisposed to taking shortcuts? "Lose twenty pounds in three days!" "Five easy steps to winning negotiations!" "Make six figures from working at home!" We laugh as we look at these obviously impossible outcomes, but sometimes we find ourselves walking down these paths. King David says in the above stanza, "Give me life according to your rules." Father God has set up a way to live that brings glory and honor to His name, regardless of the outcomes. Sometimes bad things happen to good people; we all understand that. Life is hard, but it doesn't mean that it has to be empty or without purpose. When we follow the ways of God, we will reap the fruit of those godly decisions. I am so grateful that the Lord granted me mercy my freshman year when I tried to make a quick buck. I could have easily lost the entire investment of $200. It became a lesson that I never forgot, and I have sought to live from this principle:

"Do not let greed rule your decisions."

Selah.

Journal

When was a time in your life that you allowed greed to dictate your decision? What was the outcome?

How have you overcome greed in your life?

Prayer

Father God, thank You for Your example of a generous heart. Forgive me when I allow greed to influence my decisions. Fill me with the joy of giving. You said it's better to give than to receive. May I live from this Kingdom truth all the days of my life.

In the Name of Jesus!

Hebrew Treasure
Thomas L. Boehm

Resh ר

Have you heard of the Jewish New Year? This fall festival goes by the traditional name of Rosh Hashanah, literally meaning head of the year. The Hebrew word for head is rosh (ראש) which begins with the Hebrew letter resh (ר). The last verse in this stanza begins with the Hebrew word rosh but rather than describing only a part, the translation of rosh implies the whole of God's word being truth. Some versions translate verse 160 "The sum of your word" (ASV, ESV, NASB) or "All your words" (NIV) but others translate rosh as beginning, "Thy word is true from the beginning" (KJV). The rosh or head of the year is the beginning of a year when the annual cycle begins again. Similarly, Rosh Chodesh in Hebrew literally means "head of the month" and refers to a new moon. The rosh or head of the month is the beginning of the month when the smallest sliver of the new moon appears in the sky. The idea of rosh is that the beginning connects to the end, the first connects to the last. The first day of a month or year is connected to the end of that timeframe. The beginning of God's word connects to the end. The first connects to the last. Jesus describes Himself as the alpha and the omega (the first and last letters of the Greek alphabet), "The First and the Last, the Beginning and the End" (Rev. 22:13). He also declared Himself the head (rosh) of the church. He was describing His irrevocable connection with His people. Paul explained that Jesus is "the head of the body, the church; he is the beginning and the firstborn from among the dead, so that in everything he might have the supremacy" (Col. 1:18).

Sin & Shin - Worship with the Word - "Your Word, My Treasure" by Joseph Maloney

DAY 21

The Psalm 119 Journey

ש

Sin and Shin

161 Princes persecute me without cause,
   but my heart stands in awe of your words.

162 I rejoice at your word
   like one who finds great spoil.

163 I hate and abhor falsehood,
   but I love your law.

164 Seven times a day I praise you
   for your righteous rules.

165 Great peace have those who love your law;
   nothing can make them stumble.

166 I hope for your salvation, O Lord,
   and I do your commandments.

167 My soul keeps your testimonies;
   I love them exceedingly.

168 I keep your precepts and testimonies,
   for all my ways are before you.

The Days of My Youth
God's peace is greater than my fear;
the Living Word of God leads me to that peace.

I crouched underneath my desk with my hands over my head. I looked around and saw all of my classmates in the same position. Fear marked the face of a girl to my right. Once a month, we had air-raid drills at Seoul Foreign School (SFS) in the heart of South Korea's capital. The year was 1974, and North and South Korea were still in a state of war. In my youthful innocence, I felt free and at peace even with the threat of attack from the north. How could this be?

I grew up in the Land of the Morning Calm,[83] in Seoul, South Korea, the son of missionary parents Sid and Jennetta Allen. I was blessed to grow up in a family that loved the Lord and sought to share His love. As a young boy, I attended SFS with my older brother and sister.

Each morning, my mother would rise before dawn to make a hot breakfast. We would sit down at the table to my father leading us in a devotional. It was simple. We each took turns reading from one of the gospels, and then my father would lead us in prayer. My Uncle Rand would pick us up in a late '60s International Harvester truck that in my young mind could fit twenty people.[84] Our next-door neighbors, the Parsley kids, would ride with us, and

---

[83] In the year 1934, Korea was given the title "Chaohsien" which meant morning freshness. The title was well suited to Korea because of its natural beauty of stunning mountains, clear waters and splendid peacefulness – particularly in the morning. Because of this, Korea was also called "Land of Morning Calm." Canada, Veterans Affairs. "Land of the Morning Calm and the Fragility of Peace." Veterans Affairs Canada, Government of Canada, 24 Feb. 2022, www.veterans.gc.ca/eng/remembrance/information-for/educators/learning-modules/korean-war/handout-land-of-the-morning-calm.

[84] "If I remember correctly, the faded tan International panel truck had windows all around, with custom-made couch benches in the back that could accommodate a half-dozen adults and probably up to a dozen kids. No seatbelts, 3-speed on the column; drafty but resonated with praise as we sung our way down the Kimpo Highway to Seoul Foreign School." - Rand Chesshir

Uncle Rand would lead us in worship songs from the Jesus Movement. Looking back, it was a little bit of heaven on earth.

The Apostle Paul exhorts fathers in the book of Ephesians to bring up their children in the training and instruction of the Lord.[85] Three thousand years ago, King Solomon spoke this proverb to his own sons that has echoed through the halls of time:

"Train up a child in the way he should go, and when he is old, he will not depart from it."[86]

Beloved, my parents gave me a rich gift in my youth, a love for the Word of God, and to this day at the age of fifty-six, I have not departed from it. In this fertile soil, my hunger has birthed a desire to pursue Him and His Word. It has transformed my heart and forged my character in a way that no textbook or self-improvement manual has ever done. The Word of God, planted in my heart as a youth, created an atmosphere of peace in me that was greater than the threat of war around me. What is so powerful about the Word of God?

> "Great peace have those who love your law;
>
> nothing can make them stumble."
>
> Psalm 119:165 ESV

As a child growing up in the shadow of the constant threat of war, I was at peace. How was that possible? It was through the powerful Word of the Living God who shaped me, and who is shaping you, who guided me, and who is guiding you. In His Word is His presence, and in His presence are

---

[85] Ephesians 6:4 NIV
[86] Proverbs 22:6 NIV

freedom, peace, and joy eternal. Selah.

Journal

When was the last time you responded to a potential fearful situation with peace? How were you able to do this?

How can you grow in peace?

* Follow this QR code to listen to the song, "Land Of The Morning Calm" by Rand Chesshir

Prayer

Abba Father, thank You that Your Son Jesus is the Prince of Peace. Thank You that in the midst of international political tension and the threat of war, we can still walk in peace. Thank You that peace is not the absence of conflict, but rather Your presence.

In the Name of Jesus!

Hebrew Treasure

Thomas L. Boehm

Sin and Shin ש

In Hebrew, the words for hello, goodbye, and peace are all the same word — Shalom (שָׁלוֹם) that begins with the second to last letter sin/shin (ש). Verse 165 begins with this word carrying the sense of peace. More than that, a great or abundant peace, shalom rav. In this verse, almost in the middle of the stanza, David connects this abundant peace to loving God's law. Surrounding this verse, David overflows with other descriptions of the fruits of God's spirit accessible through a heart turned to God in faith. Specifically, David's "heart stands in awe" of God's words (v. 161), he "rejoice(s)" at God's word (v. 162), is filled with "love" for God's law (v. 163), and overflows with "praise" for God's righteous rules no less than seven times a day (v. 164). Furthermore, David is anchored with "hope" for God's salvation (v. 166) and filled with "exceeding love" for God's testimonies (v. 167). I want these descriptions to characterize my day today! It reminds me of Jesus' invitation into abundant peace in Matthew 11:28-29: "Come to Me, all who are weary and heavy-laden, and I will give you rest...you will find rest for your souls." What the Father offers you and me in the power of the Holy Spirit, through following His Son, the greater David, the Messiah and King Jesus, is abundant peace. Peace and rest in our souls. But God is at work redeeming our big world, not just our small selves. There is a traditional Jewish prayer in the Ashkenazic tradition, called Shalom Rav (abundant peace), put to beautiful music in the Reform tradition. I actually sang this song at my Bar Mitzvah. The song is a prayer for God to put His abundant peace on Israel, His people, forever. God desires that your heart be filled with abundant peace today. But God has also commanded us to "pray for the peace (shalom) of Jerusalem" (Ps. 122:6) and to "give Him no rest until He establishes Jerusalem and makes her the praise of the earth" (Isa. 62:7)!

Taw - Worship with the Word - "Sing Your Word"
by Mark Woodward

DAY 22

The Psalm 119 Journey

ת

Taw

169 Let my cry come before you, O Lord;
  give me understanding according to your word!

170 Let my plea come before you;
  deliver me according to your word.

171 My lips will pour forth praise,
  for you teach me your statutes.

172 My tongue will sing of your word,
  for all your commandments are right.

173 Let your hand be ready to help me,
  for I have chosen your precepts.

174 I long for your salvation, O Lord,
  and your law is my delight.

175 Let my soul live and praise you,
  and let your rules help me.

176 I have gone astray like a lost sheep; seek your servant,
  for I do not forget your commandments.

Border Crossing
The Ancient of Days is the same today.
The One who parted the sea is the One who still makes the way.

The Thai immigration official walked out of his office, holding our four passports. Throwing them on the ground in front of our feet, he spoke loudly in Thai for everyone within earshot to hear:

"You're not going in."

I don't know who was more startled, myself or my three teammates. A few weeks before, Utan, a Cambodian member of our church in Bangkok, Thailand, had told us about an orphanage in Sisophon, Cambodia, needing food and children's school supplies. We had only been in Thailand a few years and did not know correct procedure for travel into Cambodia. We had simply prayed and felt like we were supposed to go to encourage the orphans and the director of the orphanage, a Cambodian woman named Mrs. Fisher.[87] Mrs. Fisher was married to a high-ranking Cambodian official during the horrific civil war of the mid-1970s. Her husband was killed by the communist Khmer Rouge. She fled to the United States to seek political asylum and ended up marrying a retired American Army officer. He later passed, and with the pension she received from her husband, she returned to Cambodia to help with the war orphans. At almost seventy years old, with width nearly equal to her height, she was not a woman to trifle with. Due to her girth, her knees were arthritic after years of weight-bearing. She hobbled more than walked, her face tense with pain.

The day before, we had driven from Bangkok to Aranyaprathet on the Thai-Cambodian border and spent the night at a guest house. The next morning we drove to the border crossing to meet Mrs. Fisher. Utan was acting as our guide for the trip. Mrs. Fisher carried dual passports from Cambodia and America, allowing her to travel freely across the border. The Thai-Cambodian relations had not been civil for quite a while. When we first arrived at the border crossing, we went into an immigration office to talk to

---

[87] Not her real name.

the officials about going into Cambodia for the day to visit the orphanage.

"Don't you know that you have to go to the Cambodian embassy in Bangkok and ask for a visa?" the ranking officer laughed.

"Uhh…we didn't know," we responded sheepishly. "We thought we could just drive across the border."

He sized us up for a minute, looking us over silently as he puffed on a cigarette. Finally he said, "Here are my terms. I'll keep your passports as collateral, and you must be back by 5:00 p.m. this evening. This will guarantee that you will not stay overnight in Cambodia. That is, if you want your passports back," he smiled.

"Thank you, sir. We will talk to our friends and get back to you here in a few minutes."

We walked out of the immigration office to confer with Mrs. Fisher and Utan.

"NO, you can't go across the border without your U.S. passports," Mrs. Fisher exclaimed. "The Cambodian military will not allow us across."

The Thai officer, overhearing our conversation, walked out of his office and threw our passports on the ground. Not happy with Mrs. Fisher's response, he turned around, slamming the door. I thought to myself, Well, this ended up being a short trip. I guess it's time to go back home to Bangkok. But before I knew it, Russ Pennington, one of my teammates, kneeled and started to pray. I nervously dropped to join Russ and my teammates, feeling self-conscious in the middle of this bustling border crossing.

"The Lord will make a way where there is not a way…" Russ began to play on his guitar. Slowly I started to worship until a few minutes later I found myself fully engaged, our song now a prayer.

"Look at those missionaries. There's no way they're getting across the border," laughed the armed soldiers.

Time seemed to move slowly as the morning mist burned off the rice fields around the border post, and the sun began to beat down on the tin roof. Our foreheads began to sweat as the humidity inched upward along with the heat. After several hours of intercession and worship, the door swung open and the Thai official came out.

"I've changed my mind. You can go in as long as we agree that I will keep your passports until you come back this afternoon."

"Thank you ,sir. We appreciate your help," Russ responded, jumping up with a big grin. We crossed over the border, negotiated with the Cambodian officials, and found ourselves bumping down potholed dirt roads on our way to Sisophon. The trip turned out to be amazing as we arrived at the orphanage and had the opportunity to share Jesus through Utan, who was not only our guide, but our translator. We spoke in Thai, and he translated into Cambodian for the kids. Later that afternoon, my teammates assisted Mrs. Fisher up a wooden ladder and baptized her in a large urn designed for catching the monsoon rains.

Driving back to the Thai border, I reflected on this powerful experience. We serve the same God today who parted the Red Sea 3,500 years ago, I thought to myself. God made a way where there had been no way. He opened up the border so that we could share the Gospel with a Cambodian woman with bad knees. She received the gift of salvation, and I received the gift of greater faith.

Beloved, like the Psalmist, my teammates and I had cried out to the Lord. On the border, we experienced His deliverance and responded with praise. Selah.

> "Let my plea come before you;
> deliver me according to your word.
> My lips will pour forth praise,
> for you teach me your statutes."

Psalm 119:170-171 ESV

Journal

Think back to a time when you needed deliverance. How did God make a way for you? In remembering, lift Him up in praise.

Prayer

Father God, thank You for Your deliverance. You truly are the God who makes a way where there is no way. I worship You with all my heart, soul, mind, and strength. You are worthy of it all.

In the Name of Jesus!

*Scan the QR code to listen to the song, "The Lord Will Make A Way" by Russ Pennington

Hebrew Treasure
Thomas L. Boehm

Taw ת

This final stanza of Psalm 119 connects us back to the beginning of the psalm. The very first verse of the first stanza pointed us to the blessings of joyful satisfaction (ashrei) when walking "in the law of the LORD" (v. 1). The final verse in this psalm points us to the uncomfortable reality that we tend to wander and stray like lost sheep (v. 176). The first Hebrew word in verse 176 is Ta'ee-tee (תָּעִיתִי), meaning I have gone astray, and begins with the letter Hebrew taw (ת). This tendency to stray, even with the best of intentions, is David's honest admission of his weakness along with a precious and unashamed cry for help. Thankfully, God is an ever present help when we call upon Him. David had learned this lesson and in another psalm wrote that "The LORD is near to all who call on Him, to all who call on Him in truth" (Ps. 145:18). In the first verse of this final stanza of Psalm 119, David cries out for help, "Let my cry come before you, O Lord" followed by a request for God to "give me understanding according to Your word" (v. 169). Long after David had died, God declared through the prophet Isaiah that "We all, like sheep, have gone astray, each of us has turned to his own way" (Isa. 53:6). Furthermore, through the prophet Ezekiel, God declared He would send one like David to shepherd God's people who naturally stray (Ez. 34:23). Jesus declared Himself to be that greater David, the Good Shepherd (Jn. 10:11), and the One who will always answer our cry when we cry out like David at the end of this psalm, "Seek your servant, for I do not forget your commandments" (Ps. 119:176). May His good shepherding be magnified in our straying as we surrender and submit for His glory and our good!

APPENDIX

Good News!

My friend, I have been praying for you this past year, that through this devotional, you would be drawn to the Son of the Living God. He is the Savior of the world and the Giver of life. All of history and science point toward Him. The Word of God says that all men have sinned and have fallen short of the glory of God (Romans 3:23). I made a decision in my youth to follow Jesus and to receive Him as Lord of my life. He washed away my sins and gave me eternal life. There is no other way to the Heavenly Father but through the Son, Jesus Christ. The most important decision you will ever make in your life is your decision for Christ Jesus. I invite you to read these Scriptures, confess your sins to Him, and receive Him as Savior. No treasure on this earth compares to Him. He is the Pearl of great price.

> For God so loved the world that he gave his one and only Son, that whoever believes in him shall not perish but have eternal life. For God did not send his Son into the world to condemn the world, but to save the world through him. Whoever believes in him is not condemned, but whoever does not believe stands condemned already because they have not believed in the name of God's one and only Son. This is the verdict: Light has come into the world, but people loved darkness instead of light because their deeds were evil. Everyone who does evil hates the light, and will not come into the light for fear that their deeds will be exposed. But whoever lives by the truth comes into the light, so that it may be seen plainly that what they have done has been done in the sight of God.

John 3:16-21 NIV

If you declare with your mouth, "Jesus is Lord," and believe in your heart that God raised him from the dead, you will be saved. For it is with your heart that you believe and are justified, and it is with your mouth that you profess your faith and are saved. As Scripture says, "Anyone who believes in him will never be put to shame." For there is no difference between Jew and Gentile — the same Lord is Lord of all and richly blesses all who call on him, for, "Everyone who calls on the name of the Lord will be saved."

Romans 10:9-13 NIV

Salvation is found in no one else, for there is no other name under heaven given to mankind by which we must be saved.

Acts 4:12 NIV

If you are ready to receive Jesus Christ as Lord of your life, pray this prayer out loud with me:

> Jesus, I confess that I am a sinner and cannot save myself. Thank You that You gave Your life for me on the cross. I receive You as Lord and Savior of my life, and I surrender myself to You, that I would follow You with all my heart, soul, mind, and strength for the rest of my life. I am not saved by my good works. By the blood that You shed on the cross, I receive Your atonement. It is through Your death, burial, and resurrection that I receive new life. Thank You, Jesus, that You have saved me.

Congratulations, my friend! You now belong to Him. Your next step is to find a local church that believes in the Word of God and is filled with the Holy Spirit. As an act of obedience, be baptized in water according to the Scriptures — Acts 2:38. In this journey of faith, you will encounter obstacles, but be encouraged. The Lord will give you everything you need for this new life.

Repeat with me:

I am His! I am forgiven! I am accepted! I belong!

STORING PSALM 119 IN YOUR HEART

> "And the words of the Lord are flawless, like silver refined in a furnace of clay, purified seven times."
>
> Psalm 12:6 NIV 1984

Seven Steps to Memorizing Psalm 119:

1. Develop a plan - example: fifteen minutes a day for five days a week.
2. Have soaking or instrumental worship in the background as you are memorizing. This helps you to remember the Word. Listen to Psalm 119 being sung via the QR codes on each devotional.
3. Write out the Word - use an index card for each stanza of eight verses.
4. Partner with a friend in the Psalm 119 memorization journey (Ecclesiastes 4:9-12).
5. Each day, ask the Holy Spirit to write the Word of God on your heart (Psalm 119:9-11).
6. Visualization - create a picture in your mind for each of the seven synonyms for the Word of God
(law, testimonies, precepts, statutes, commandments, rules, and word). Use this technique for other words you want to remember.
7. Set a date to complete the memorization of Psalm 119, and then celebrate by going out to your favorite restaurant or taking a special trip.

"There's no such thing as a bad memory or a good memory, just a trained memory."
Jim Kwik

Psalm 119

The Jesus Psalm
Jesus Is a Lamp to My Feet
ישוע הוא מנורה לרגלי
By Steve Allen under the inspiration of the Holy Spirit

א Aleph

1 Blessed are those whose way is blameless,
   who walk in **Jesus**!
2 Blessed are those who keep **Jesus**,
   who seek Him with their whole heart,
3 who also do no wrong,
   but walk in **Jesus**!
4 You have commanded **Jesus**
   to be kept diligently.
5 Oh that my ways may be steadfast
   in keeping **Jesus**!
6 Then I shall not be put to shame,
   having my eyes fixed on **Jesus**.
7 I will praise you with an upright heart,
   when I learn **Jesus**.
8 I will keep **Jesus**;
   do not utterly forsake me!

ב Beth

9 How can a young man keep his way pure?
   By guarding it according to **Jesus**.
10 With my whole heart I seek you;
   let me not wander from **Jesus**!
11 I have stored up **Jesus** in my heart,
   that I might not sin against you.
12 Blessed are you, O Lord;

teach me **Jesus**!
13 With my lips I declare
   Jesus.
14 In the way of **Jesus** I delight
   as much as in all riches.
15 I will meditate on **Jesus**
   and fix my eyes on Him.
16 I will delight in **Jesus**;
   I will not forget Him.

ג **Gimel**

17 Deal bountifully with your servant,
   that I may live and keep **Jesus**.
18 Open my eyes, that I may behold
   wondrous things in **Jesus**.
19 I am a sojourner on the earth;
   hide not **Jesus** from me!
20 My soul is consumed with longing
   for **Jesus** at all times.
21 You rebuke the insolent, accursed ones,
   who wander from **Jesus**.
22 Take away from me scorn and contempt,
   for I have kept **Jesus**.
23 Even though princes sit plotting against me,
   your servant will meditate on **Jesus**.
24 **Jesus** is my delight;
   He is my counselor.

ד **Daleth**

25 My soul clings to the dust;
   give me life according to **Jesus**!
26 When I told of my ways, you answered me;

teach me **Jesus**!
27 Make me understand the way of **Jesus**,
    and I will meditate on your wondrous works.
28 My soul melts away for sorrow;
    strengthen me according to **Jesus**!
29 Put false ways far from me
    and graciously teach me **Jesus**!
30 I have chosen the way of faithfulness;
    I set **Jesus** before me.
31 I cling to **Jesus**, O Lord;
    let me not be put to shame!
32 I will run in the way of **Jesus**
    when you enlarge my heart!

ה **He**

33 Teach me, O Lord, the way of **Jesus**;
    and I will keep Him to the end.
34 Give me understanding, that I may keep **Jesus**
    and observe Him with my whole heart.
35 Lead me in the path of **Jesus**,
    for I delight in Him.
36 Incline my heart to **Jesus**,
    and not to selfish gain!
37 Turn my eyes from looking at worthless things;
    and give me life in **Jesus**.
38 Confirm **Jesus** to your servant,
    that you may be feared.
39 Turn away the reproach that I dread,
    for **Jesus** is good.
40 Behold, I long for **Jesus**;
    in your righteousness give me life!

ו Waw

41 Let your steadfast love come to me, O Lord,
   your salvation according to **Jesus**;
42 then shall I have an answer for him who taunts me,
   for I trust in **Jesus**.
43 And take not **Jesus** utterly out of my mouth,
   for my hope is in Him.
44 I will keep **Jesus** continually,
   forever and ever,
45 and I shall walk in a wide place,
   for I have sought **Jesus**.
46 I will also speak of **Jesus** before kings
   and shall not be put to shame,
47 for I find my delight in **Jesus**,
   whom I love.
48 I will lift up my hands toward **Jesus**, whom I love,
   and I will meditate on Him.

ז Zayin

49 Remember **Jesus** to your servant,
   in whom you have made me hope.
50 This is my comfort in my affliction,
   that **Jesus** gives me life.
51 The insolent utterly deride me,
   but I do not turn away from **Jesus**.
52 When I think of **Jesus** from of old,
   I take comfort, O Lord.
53 Hot indignation seizes me because of the wicked,
   who forsake **Jesus**.
54 **Jesus** has been my song
   in the house of my sojourning.
55 I remember your name in the night, O Lord,

and keep **Jesus**.
56 This blessing has fallen to me,
    that I have kept **Jesus**.

ח **Heth**

57 The Lord is my portion;
    I promise to keep **Jesus**.
58 I entreat your favor with all my heart;
    be gracious to me according to **Jesus**.
59 When I think on my ways,
    I turn my feet to **Jesus**;
60 I hasten and do not delay
    to keep **Jesus**.
61 Though the cords of the wicked ensnare me,
    I do not forget **Jesus**.
62 At midnight I rise to praise you,
    because of **Jesus**.
63 I am a companion of all who fear you,
    of those who keep **Jesus**.
64 The earth, O Lord, is full of your steadfast love;
    teach me **Jesus**!

ט **Teth**

65 You have dealt well with your servant,
    O Lord, according to **Jesus**.
66 Teach me good judgment and knowledge,
    for I believe in **Jesus**.
67 Before I was afflicted I went astray,
    but now I keep **Jesus**.
68 You are good and do good;
    teach me **Jesus**.
69 The insolent smear me with lies,

   but with my whole heart I keep **Jesus**;
70 their heart is unfeeling like fat,
   but I delight in **Jesus**.
71 It is good for me that I was afflicted,
   that I might learn **Jesus**.
72 **Jesus** is better to me
   than thousands of gold and silver pieces.

׳ Yodh

73 Your hands have made and fashioned me;
   give me understanding that I may learn **Jesus**.
74 Those who fear you shall see me and rejoice,
   because I have hoped in **Jesus**.
75 I know, O Lord, that **Jesus** is righteous,
   and that in faithfulness you have afflicted me.
76 Let your steadfast love comfort me
   according to your promise of **Jesus** to your servant.
77 Let your mercy come to me, that I may live;
   for **Jesus** is my delight.
78 Let the insolent be put to shame,
   because they have wronged me with falsehood;
   as for me, I will meditate on **Jesus**.
79 Let those who fear you turn to me,
   that they may know **Jesus**.
80 May my heart be blameless in **Jesus**,
   that I may not be put to shame!

כ Kaph

81 My soul longs for your salvation;
   I hope in **Jesus**.
82 My eyes long for **Jesus**;
   I ask, "When will you comfort me?"

83 For I have become like a wineskin in the smoke,
  yet I have not forgotten **Jesus**.
84 How long must your servant endure?
  When will you judge those who persecute me?
85 The insolent have dug pitfalls for me;
  they do not live according to **Jesus**.
86 **Jesus** is sure;
  they persecute me with falsehood; help me!
87 They have almost made an end of me on earth,
  but I have not forsaken **Jesus**.
88 In your steadfast love give me life,
  that I may keep **Jesus**.

ל Lamedh

89 Forever, O Lord, **Jesus**
  is firmly fixed in the heavens.
90 Your faithfulness endures to all generations;
  you have established the earth, and it stands fast.
91 By your appointment they stand this day,
  for all things are your servants.
92 If **Jesus** had not been my delight,
  I would have perished in my affliction.
93 I will never forget **Jesus**,
  for by Him you have given me life.
94 I am yours; save me,
  for I have sought **Jesus**.
95 The wicked lie in wait to destroy me,
  but I consider **Jesus**.
96 I have seen a limit to all perfection,
  but **Jesus** is exceedingly broad.

מ Mem

97 Oh how I love **Jesus**!
   He is my meditation all the day.
98 **Jesus** makes me wiser than my enemies,
   for He is ever with me.
99 I have more understanding than all my teachers,
   for **Jesus** is my meditation.
100 I understand more than the aged,
   for I keep **Jesus**.
101 I hold back my feet from every evil way,
   in order to keep **Jesus**.
102 I do not turn aside from **Jesus**,
   for you have taught me.
103 How sweet is **Jesus** to my taste,
   sweeter than honey to my mouth!
104 Through **Jesus** I get understanding;
   therefore I hate every false way.

נ Nun

105 **Jesus** is a lamp to my feet
   and a light to my path.
106 I have sworn an oath and confirmed it,
   to keep **Jesus**.
107 I am severely afflicted;
   give me life, O Lord, according to **Jesus**!
108 Accept my freewill offerings of praise, O Lord,
   and teach me **Jesus**.
109 I hold my life in my hand continually,
   but I do not forget **Jesus**.
110 The wicked have laid a snare for me,
   but I do not stray from **Jesus**.
111 **Jesus** is my heritage forever,

for He is the joy of my heart.
112 I incline my heart to follow **Jesus**
forever, to the end.

ס Samekh

113 I hate the double-minded,
but I love **Jesus**.
114 You are my hiding place and my shield;
I hope in **Jesus**.
115 Depart from me, you evildoers,
that I may keep the **Jesus** of my God.
116 Uphold me according to **Jesus**, that I may live,
and let me not be put to shame in my hope!
117 Hold me up, that I may be safe
and have regard for **Jesus** continually!
118 You spurn all who go astray from **Jesus**,
for their cunning is in vain.
119 All the wicked of the earth you discard like dross,
therefore I love **Jesus**.
120 My flesh trembles for fear of you,
and I fear **Jesus**.

ע Ayin

121 I have done what is just and right;
do not leave me to my oppressors.
122 Give your servant a pledge of good;
let not the insolent oppress me.
123 My eyes long for your salvation
and for the fulfillment of **Jesus**.
124 Deal with your servant according to your steadfast love,
and teach me **Jesus**.
125 I am your servant; give me understanding,

that I may know **Jesus**!
126 It is time for the Lord to act,
   for **Jesus** has been broken.
127 Therefore I love **Jesus**
   above gold, above fine gold.
128 Therefore I consider all of **Jesus** to be right;
   I hate every false way.

פ Pe

129 **Jesus** is wonderful;
   therefore my soul keeps Him.
130 The unfolding of **Jesus** gives light;
   He imparts understanding to the simple.
131 I open my mouth and pant,
   because I long for **Jesus**.
132 Turn to me and be gracious to me,
   as is **Jesus** with those who love your name.
133 Keep steady my steps according to **Jesus**,
   and let no iniquity get dominion over me.
134 Redeem me from man's oppression,
   that I may keep **Jesus**.
135 Make your face shine upon your servant,
   and teach me **Jesus**.
136 My eyes shed streams of tears,
   because people do not keep **Jesus**.

צ Tsadhe

137 Righteous are you, O Lord,
   and right is **Jesus**.
138 You have appointed **Jesus** in righteousness
   and in all faithfulness.
139 My zeal consumes me,

THE PSALM 119 JOURNEY

because my foes forget **Jesus**.
140 **Jesus** is well tried,
and your servant loves Him.
141 I am small and despised,
yet I do not forget **Jesus**.
142 Your righteousness is righteous forever,
and **Jesus** is true.
143 Trouble and anguish have found me out,
but **Jesus** is my delight.
144 **Jesus** is righteous forever;
give me understanding that I may live.

ק Qoph

145 With my whole heart I cry; answer me, O Lord!
I will keep **Jesus**.
146 I call to you; save me,
that I may observe **Jesus**.
147 I rise before dawn and cry for help;
I hope in **Jesus**.
148 My eyes are awake before the watches of the night,
that I may meditate on **Jesus**.
149 Hear my voice according to your steadfast love;
O Lord, according to **Jesus** give me life.
150 They draw near who persecute me with evil purpose;
they are far from **Jesus**.
151 But you are near, O Lord,
and **Jesus** is true.
152 Long have I known from **Jesus**
that you have founded Him forever.

ר Resh

153 Look on my affliction and deliver me,
   for I do not forget **Jesus**.
154 Plead my cause and redeem me;
   give me life according to **Jesus**!
155 Salvation is far from the wicked,
   for they do not seek **Jesus**.
156 Great is your mercy, O Lord;
   give me life according to **Jesus**.
157 Many are my persecutors and my adversaries,
   but I do not swerve from **Jesus**.
158 I look at the faithless with disgust,
   because they do not keep **Jesus**.
159 Consider how I love **Jesus**!
   Give me life according to your steadfast love.
160 The sum of **Jesus** is truth,
   and **Jesus** endures forever.

ש Sin and Shin

161 Princes persecute me without cause,
   but my heart stands in awe of **Jesus**.
162 I rejoice in **Jesus**
   like one who finds great spoil.
163 I hate and abhor falsehood,
   but I love **Jesus**.
164 Seven times a day I praise you
   for **Jesus**.
165 Great peace have those who love **Jesus**;
   nothing can make them stumble.
166 I hope for your salvation, O Lord,
   and I follow **Jesus**.
167 My soul keeps **Jesus**;

I love Him exceedingly.
168 I keep **Jesus**
for all my ways are before you.

ת **Taw**

169 Let my cry come before you, O Lord;
give me understanding according to **Jesus**!
170 Let my plea come before you;
deliver me according to **Jesus**.
171 My lips will pour forth praise,
for you teach me **Jesus**.
172 My tongue will sing of **Jesus**,
for He is right.
173 Let your hand be ready to help me,
for I have chosen **Jesus**.
174 I long for your salvation, O Lord,
and **Jesus** is my delight.
175 Let my soul live and praise you,
and let **Jesus** help me.
176 I have gone astray like a lost sheep; seek your servant,
for I do not forget Jesus.

My Psalm 119 Journey Testimonial
Joseph Maloney

Psalm 119 is a chapter of the Bible that might as well be its own book. When God puts this chapter on your heart and starts drawing you into it, it slowly but surely becomes all- encompassing. Before you know it, it becomes your world and turns into a godly obsession that culminates in a passionate love for the Word of God.

My journey with Psalm 119 started around the time I met Steve Allen. I heard him propose a question and it took root in me – "If you were to find yourself in a prison being persecuted for the Gospel but could not have a Bible with you, what three chapters would you want to have stored in your heart?" I love the phrase "store in heart" rather than "memorize" because sometimes "memorize" can sound like a religious obligation, where to store something in your heart involves love and a relationship. My initial response to this question was Romans 8, Psalm 91, and Matthew 5. Somewhere in- between getting Psalm 91 in my heart and Romans 8, I had the thought:

If I can store all of Psalm 119 in my heart, the longest chapter in the Bible, then I can store anything in my heart!

So, the adventure began!

Storing the Word in my heart was never something that came naturally. In fact, in the past I would have been the person who would say that I couldn't do it. I thought it was supposed to happen naturally, that some people either had the spiritual or cognitive trait and others didn't, myself included. However, in 2019, God put a scripture on my heart and said to me, "Joseph, as you store this chapter in your heart it will become a reality in your life." The chapter was Isaiah 61, the scripture that Jesus declares over himself when He starts his ministry after coming out of the wilderness, fasting for 40 days. So, I did just that. I stored it in my heart and my year was radically marked by Isaiah 61, the year of the Lord's Favor. Instead of trying to get 2-5 verses inside of me every day, I felt the Holy Spirit slowing me down and leading me to a single verse daily, to focus more on consistency and depth.

Around this time, I stumbled upon a book called Seven Men written by Eric Metaxas. This book shared the life stories of seven men who changed the course of history, one being a man named William Wilberforce, whom I knew nothing about. In reading, I learned that Wilberforce was the man most responsible for ending the slave trade in the early 1800's. He was the youngest member of the English Parliament and would walk through Hyde Park every day on his way to work reciting all of Psalm 119 from his heart. It took him roughly 20 minutes to speak the whole chapter. I connected the dots; this man had such a heart for God's justice and also meditated on this beautiful masterpiece of scripture regularly. On my initial attempt to store Psalm 119 in my heart, I did it alone and was able to get to He, the fifth Hebrew letter, before losing motivation and giving up.

Several months after this I was spending time with a spiritual father of mine named Don Finto and was talking to him about how to store the Word of God in your heart. He dropped a nugget of wisdom that changed my approach to Psalm 119, which helped get me back on the horse. He said, "Joseph, when you are storing a large section of scripture in your heart, it is best to do it like a musician would learn a long orchestral piece – you start at the end and work towards the beginning." Two things impacted me from this conversation, starting from the end of Psalm 119 and working towards the beginning, and then secondly was to sing it! So, I began round two. This time I made it from the last section Taw to the 14th section – Nun. However, once again I lost motivation and stopped. To say getting Psalm 119 stored in your heart is a marathon is an understatement. I learned one of the most important lessons about storing the Word inside me during this time: when you sing it, scripture goes from two-dimensional to three-dimensional and gets solidified in a deeper part of your being than just repeating the words without melody.

Shortly after I visited Colorado Springs for a prayer gathering, I providentially reconnected with Steve Allen after several years of not seeing him. I had heard that he had all of Psalm 119 in his heart and it so inspired me that I shared with him about the Psalm 119 songs I was working on. He immediately lit up with excitement and said, "Joseph, I am writing a book on Psalm 119; would you be interested in partnering with me in writing the songs for the 22 sections? Pray about it!" I prayed about it and then said yes!

Steve created a group called the Psalm 119 Tribe and we all worked together to get Psalm 119 stored in our heart over the course of the next 22 weeks. On this final stretch of the journey, I picked up a book about David Livingstone at my favorite used bookstore in Nashville. David Livingstone was a medical missionary and explorer who expanded the trade route through some of the roughest parts of Africa, and he named Victoria Falls after Queen Victoria. I learned through reading that by the age of nine years old, Livingstone stored all of Psalm 119 in his heart, all 176 verses, 2,337 words!

In the following months I was finally able to complete this journey one afternoon in April while walking at Shelby Bottoms in Nashville, my favorite place to walk with the Word. That night I was at my house and around 9 pm I heard loud noises outside which I thought were gunshots. When I went out to see, I looked in the sky, and to my surprise I saw fireworks. God whispered to my spirit in that moment that He was celebrating me completing this journey. Shortly after, I visited Steve Allen in Colorado Springs for a vision trip for the book and we went up to Pikes Peak. On the drive down we spoke Psalm 119 back to each other, alternating stanzas from Aleph to Taw as we descended the mountain. It was such a special drive.

After being in Nashville, Tennessee for eight years, I felt the Lord lead me to move to Dallas, Texas. I did not have a place to stay, a job, or any significant connections, but there was a church, UPPERROOM Dallas, that I wanted to become a part of. The second day after arriving I received a text from an unknown number saying that she was someone who went to UPPERROOM and wanted to help connect me with community. She told me about a Bible study, which I attended the next day, where I met my new tribe and began to experience a depth of community that I did not have before. I later found out that Mark Woodward, the producer and one of the other songwriters for the Psalm 119 journey, had reached out to a friend of his who gave a girl named Cayla my number. So, this connection I had formed through the Psalm 119 Journey was the very thing that brought the provision for meeting my community in Dallas.

Psalm 119 has been such a rich blessing to my life. It connected me at a deeper level with Steve Allen, helped introduce me to Mark Woodward, taught me how to truly delight in the Word of God, and showed me that it is possible to get any chapter of the Bible stored in my heart no matter how long it takes. I have expectancy and anticipation that these songs and this devotional book will bring tangible change in peoples' lives, giving them a passion for the Word and delivering them from pornography, addiction, and other sin patterns.

Joseph Maloney
Dallas, Texas

My Psalm 119 Journey Testimonial
Mark Woodward

"But the Advocate, the Holy Spirit, whom the Father will send in my name, will teach you all things and will remind you of everything I have said to you." - John 14:26

"Mark this day for the Lord is going to do something great…"

The stranger's voice echoed through the large room as the astonished congregation listened with full attention.

"I have a word from the Lord that there is a couple here who has been unable to conceive, and God is going to open that woman's womb. Mark this day for the Lord is going to do something great. Go home and mark this day on your calendars…"

The stranger went on at length and then went back to his seat.

My parents were in fact the only couple in the church who couldn't have children. It had been eight years of marriage, and my parents had seen their friends have babies and start families. Like Sarai, my mom laughed. If God wanted to give me children, it would have happened already.

But my dad knew that it was God, and wept in the chair next to her.

I was born roughly 10 months later on Thanksgiving Day — November 25, 1982. I had beta strep sepsis, which carried an 80% infant fatality rate in 1982. After being in intensive care on 100% oxygen for almost a week, my mom finally got to hold me. She had never doubted that I would live, even when the doctors repeatedly communicated my slim chances.

They named me Mark. And I knew that I was a miracle, and that as such, God must have something special for me to do on earth.

Though I was a fairly religious kid and had read the Bible through by age 12, God became real to me at a Vineyard Church summer camp. So, when I struggled to make friends in the 8th grade at my new public school, and then at a private out-of-town high school, Jesus became someone that I inwardly embraced and talked to every day. As a sophomore in high school, I started reading the Bible every night.

I'm sure there was some positive effect, but it kind of went in one ear and out the other. When I went to college and my roommate challenged me to support some of my "radical" beliefs with scripture, I realized that I could not recall any of the scripture I had read!

Sometime later, I received the baptism in the Holy Spirit. For me, it was an experience that would impact the rest of my life. It was January of my freshman year at Belmont University in Nashville, and I was by myself in my dorm room reading a book my dad had given to me — A Handbook on Holy Spirit Baptism by Don Basham.

As I neared the end of the book, I started to feel the presence of God in the room. There was a movement in my stomach area and my whole body was tingling. I leaned my chair up against my bed and started to move my lips. A new language tumbled out of my mouth like a torrent. I felt like God was right in front of me and a river was pouring through my mouth and out my chest. I felt so clean. I worshiped God for a long time by myself with this new language flooding out of me. At some point, a good friend strolled in the door and was arrested by the whole story of what had happened to me. He was somewhat disturbed by what I told him but tried to be happy for me. I didn't care. I went to bed that night laughing and praising God and awoke the next morning with the joy still fresh.

I skipped a class that day so that I could sit in my room and read my Bible. I was surprised to find that it read like a new book! Things flew out at me that I had never noticed before.

Sometimes you must have an experience in God that opens your eyes to see new things in the scripture. Peter had to have the vision of the unclean animals in the sheet (Acts 10) to realize that Jesus came for the Gentiles too. Paul had to have the Road to Damascus experience before he could recognize that Jesus was the promised Messiah and Son of God. Someone who knows God will know different things about God than someone who only knows about God. For me, the Bible became a different book, and God started to use the Scripture to speak directly to me.

It was around this time that I started memorizing the Psalms and putting them to music. I was a music major in college and had written a few hundred worship songs as a young man, so putting the Psalms into music was a natural outflow of what God was doing in me.

That was 20 years ago. I am now a K-12 music teacher, married to my best friend, and we have six children. I stopped being a regular worship leader a decade ago and I write children's musicals and do household chores. A lot of dreams can be born and die in that length of time. Dreams and desires can come from the Lord, but if they are not submitted to the Lord, they can wreak havoc.

"What causes fights and quarrels among you? Don't they come from your desires that battle within you?" James 4:1

"Delight yourself in the Lord, and he will give you the desires of your heart." Psalm 37:4

We cannot serve our desires as if they were God, but God does want to give us our desires, when our number one desire is for Him!

So, I had to stop and pinch myself when Steve Allen approached me about recording the music for the Psalm 119 Project and connected me with Joseph Maloney.

Joseph is a true-hearted lover of God with a David-like psalmist gift. Musically, he is special. He does not over-think his creative process but just steps out on the water and keeps walking like a Peter who never doubted.

I keenly remember spending hours rocking our newborn Harvest Rose to sleep and singing through Yodh (Psalm 119: 73-80).

The project was nearing completion during a time that I was running for School Board in Davidson County. Educational issues had begun to loom large in my heart and mind. In early 2020, I decided that I could not sit by and watch any longer. In running for office, I came into a deeper personal connection with Psalm 119.

I cried out to God to give me the right words to speak at events, release on my website, and in public forums.

"Let my cry come before you, O Lord. Give me understanding according to your word!"
Psalm 119:169

I watched as things I said were publicly twisted and I was interrogated and ridiculed online.

"The insolent utterly deride me, but I will not turn away from your law."
Ps 119:51

I watched as a former church friend slandered me on Facebook.

"Let the insolent be put to shame, because they have wronged me with falsehood…"

Psalm 119:78

"They persecute me with falsehood, help me!"
Psalm 119:86b

I gave interviews and had conversations not knowing if I was walking in safe territory or into a trap.

"The wicked lie in wait to destroy me, but I consider your testimonies."
Psalm 119:95

I struggled to find the right words and the right tone to respond to rude emails and suspicious questions on social media.

"Let your steadfast love come to me, O Lord, Your salvation according to your promise; then shall I have an answer for him who taunts me…"
Psalm 119:41-42

I found myself with an opportunity to damage my opponent in the press, but only by bending the truth and making a mountain out of a somewhat small molehill.

"Before I was afflicted I went astray, but now I keep your word."
Psalm 119:67

"I know, O Lord, that your rules are righteous, and that in faithfulness you have afflicted me."
Psalm 119:75

Tempted with the opportunity to gain in the polls, I lost my peace for a whole week. I was emotionally and mentally afflicted. Only when I firmly told my persistent campaign manager that I would have no part in the press release did my joy come flooding back. We never went to press, and I lost by six votes in the primary. But I kept my honor and my integrity.

Something that inspires me about David is that at every turn, his heart has one response — devotion to God in keeping and meditating on His Word. We normally see commands and laws in a negative light. Think about the heart of a man who loves God's laws and says "It is good for me that I was afflicted, that I might learn your statutes." This is the man after God's own heart through whom God extended mercy to Israel and Judah over the course of their whole history. And then He let His own Son be known as the Son of David.

In closing, as you go deep in your own Psalm 119 Journey, may you catch the heart of David who caught the heart of God.

Mark Woodward
Nashville, Tennessee

Testimony on Memorizing Psalm 119
Perky Sun

The more I memorized Psalm 119, the more I noticed myself being drawn to His word! I started off the year with a new year's resolution to memorize the whole chapter by the end of the year. I started off memorizing eight verses a week but halfway through, I took a break and didn't continue. During the summer, I was reminded repeatedly to get back to it, but because it felt like such a daunting goal, I didn't do it. Finally, in October, I realized that if I did eight verses a week, I would finish the chapter by the last week of 2021! The thought of being close to finishing motivated me and I cried out for His wisdom and help to finish strong. He did it! Looking back, as I memorized, the Lord would speak to me through those exact verses I was memorizing. A few that come to mind are verses 33-40 where the author cries out for God to teach him and revive him according to His words, and that we, as His servants, would be devoted to the fear of God. Another verse that I kept going back to was verse 62, "at midnight I will rise to give thanks unto thee because of thy righteous judgments." I found myself quoting that verse in the middle of the night and giving thanks for His righteousness. Lastly, one verse that I have proclaimed a lot as I prayed for California and America is verse 142, "Thy righteousness is an everlasting righteousness, and thy law is the truth." I can rest in the truth that what happens in our nation will never alter His unchanging righteousness that lasts throughout all eternity. Praise God!

Till He Comes,
Priscilla Perky Sun

Land of the Morning Calm
by Rand Chesshir

Land of the Morning Calm shine brightly
Let every nation sing our song
I've climbed your mountains and your valleys
In your sweet hills I've talked with God

There's no other place on earth I'd rather be
Then in my home in the Land of the Morning calm

Land of the morning calm be happy
Let's show the world that we are one
I left my friends and my family
To live and share with you God's love

There's no other place on earth I'd rather be
Then in my home in the Land of the Morning calm

Land of the morning calm my brothers
Let's live in freedom live in love
And may our children share these blessings
And know the Father's Son has shone

And there's no other place on earth I'd rather be
Then in my home in the Land of Morning Calm

Rand Chesshir
Abbey Songs © 2022
최 랜드

*Scan the QR code to listen to the song, "Land of the Morning Calm" by Rand Chesshir

The Lord Will Make a Way
Russell Pennington

Chorus:
The Lord will make a way where there is not a way.
He opens up the door and lets in the light of day.
I know that we will make it. I know that we will win.
All we've got to do is keep on fighting till the end.
Verse 1
Now Moses led the people out up from Pharaoh's land.
Pharaoh didn't like it so he chased them through the sand.
Things were looking hopeless and they didn't know what to do.
The Lord He opened up the sea and led the people through.
Chorus:
The Lord will make a way where there is not a way.
He opens up the door and lets in the light of day.
I know that we will make it. I know that we will win.
All we've got to do is keep on fighting till the end.
Verse 2:
It's a few years later but our God is still the same.
He said He'd give us everything we ask in Jesus' name.
Well Lord our hearts are open as we stand before your throne.
We're asking that you build your church and make your kingdom known.
Chorus:
The Lord will make a way where there is not a way.
He opens up the door and lets in the light of day.
I know that we will make it. I know that we will win.
All we've got to do is keep on fighting till the end.

*Scan the QR code to listen to the song, "The Lord Will Make A Way" by Russ Pennington

A Sabbath Invitation
Steve Allen

My wife Samantha and I have been celebrating the Sabbath for the past 10 years, and it has had a profound impact on our lives. It is fascinating to me that when you talk to a western believer and ask which of the 10 Commandments is not relevant for today, they respond with the Sabbath. I would differ.

In 2019, The Bloomberg Global Health Index ranked the United States 35th out of all the nations in terms of health and life expectancy. The culprit? Stress and obesity. We do not know how to rest.

In January of this year, the Lord spoke quietly to my heart that He wanted the whole Sabbath on Saturdays. Previously, I would spend the morning with the Lord and then in the afternoon make calls to friends and family. The first Saturday I sought to pursue this, I got an emergency call from some good friends that took up an hour and a half of my afternoon. Later, I realized that it was not an emergency but could have been taken care of that evening or the next day.

The enemy does not want us to rest. Why? In Sabbath rest, we learn to abide in the vine. In Sabbath rest, we learn to hear His voice more clearly. The Sabbath helps us to disengage from the tyranny of the urgent and connect to the heart of Father God. In reality, the enemy is terrified of the Saints of God resting. For in resting, we find our identity, our purpose, and our renewed vision for the King and His Kingdom.

Samantha loves her Sabbaths as she spends time with the Lord, paints, takes walks, talks to friends, and usually has a hot bath. It is not religious, but relational.

My time with the Lord is different than it was before. I am more at peace now. My battle with ALS has given me a greater sense of abiding, resting, and waiting on the Lord. He truly is my life and my next breath. The Psalm 119 Journey Devotional that is in your hand is the fruit of the last three years meditating on the Word and the Word washing me with Truth and life.

The pictures you see here capture my Saturdays with the Lord. I love sitting in the front bay window of my house because I can see Pikes Peak, America's Mountain, a 14,000-footer to the west of us. I'm here from 9 in the morning until 5 in the afternoon meditating on the Word, talking to the Father, and enjoying worship. It gives me time to decompress from a busy week and think about things that are eternal.

My life verse is imprinted above the window, a gift from Samantha for my 56th birthday. It is Psalm 119:32 from the Jesus Psalm that you read in this appendix.

The writer of Hebrews says this, "Make every effort to enter into His rest." (Hebrews 4:11a) Here is the irony about the Sabbath rest: It takes focus and work to enter in.

The days ahead will get more intense and challenging. The time to prepare is not in the middle of the storm, but before it. The Father beckons to you with an invitation from the beginning of time. Take time to enter His rest this week. His invitation awaits.

Steve on his Sabbath looking at Pikes Peak

I run in the path of Jesus for He has set my heart free!

Steve's Life Verse - Psalm 119:32 - The Jesus Psalm

Pikes Peak at Sunrise

ALLEN FAMILY MINISTRIES BOOKS
ORDER ON AMAZON

WALK WITH ME

GOD'S SOLUTIONS FOR AMERICA'S *HURTING CHILDREN*

BY SAMANTHA ALLEN AND SARAH WEBB

WALK WITH ME
SAMANTHA ALLEN AND SARAH WEBB

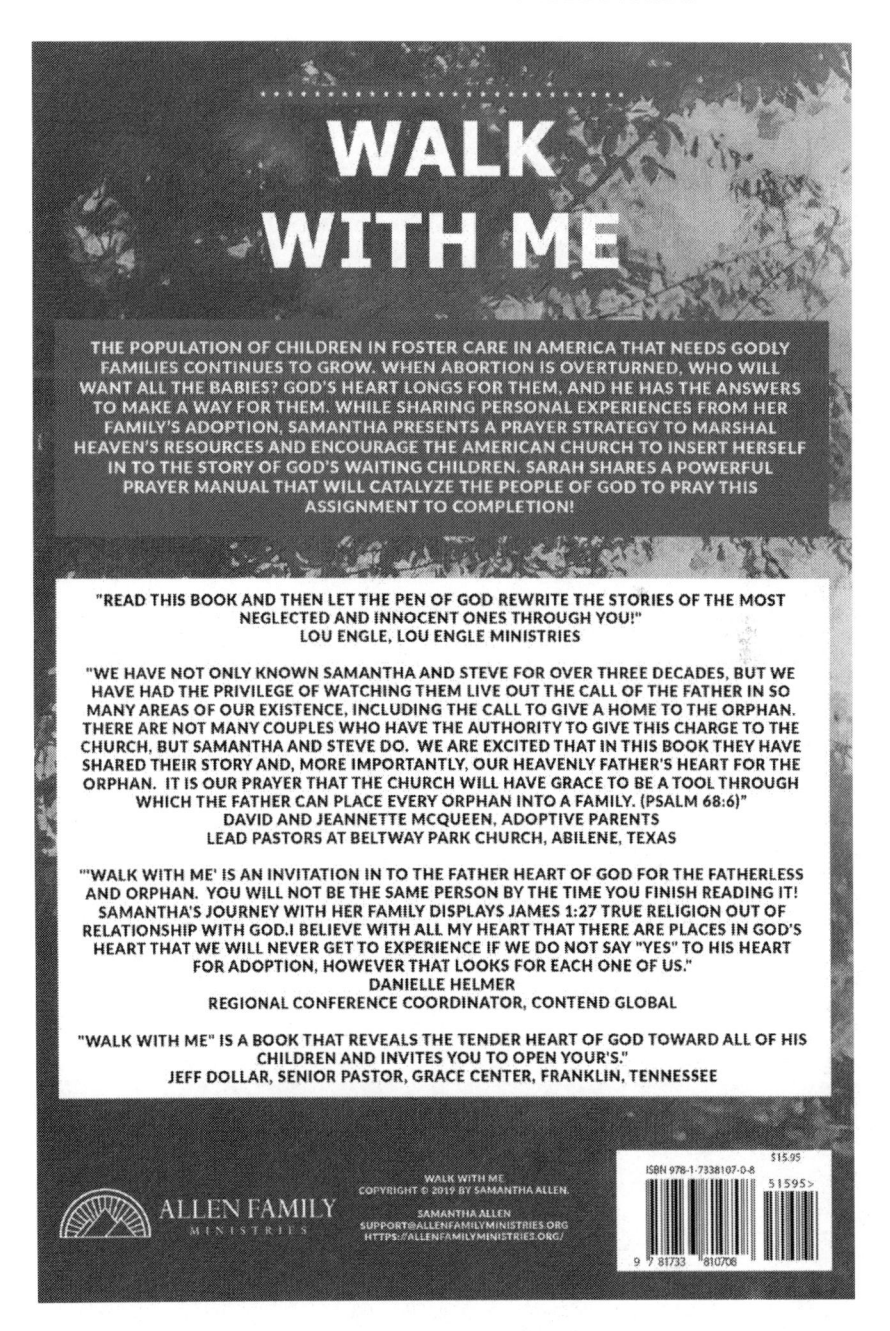

WALK WITH ME

THE POPULATION OF CHILDREN IN FOSTER CARE IN AMERICA THAT NEEDS GODLY FAMILIES CONTINUES TO GROW. WHEN ABORTION IS OVERTURNED, WHO WILL WANT ALL THE BABIES? GOD'S HEART LONGS FOR THEM, AND HE HAS THE ANSWERS TO MAKE A WAY FOR THEM. WHILE SHARING PERSONAL EXPERIENCES FROM HER FAMILY'S ADOPTION, SAMANTHA PRESENTS A PRAYER STRATEGY TO MARSHAL HEAVEN'S RESOURCES AND ENCOURAGE THE AMERICAN CHURCH TO INSERT HERSELF IN TO THE STORY OF GOD'S WAITING CHILDREN. SARAH SHARES A POWERFUL PRAYER MANUAL THAT WILL CATALYZE THE PEOPLE OF GOD TO PRAY THIS ASSIGNMENT TO COMPLETION!

"READ THIS BOOK AND THEN LET THE PEN OF GOD REWRITE THE STORIES OF THE MOST NEGLECTED AND INNOCENT ONES THROUGH YOU!"
LOU ENGLE, LOU ENGLE MINISTRIES

"WE HAVE NOT ONLY KNOWN SAMANTHA AND STEVE FOR OVER THREE DECADES, BUT WE HAVE HAD THE PRIVILEGE OF WATCHING THEM LIVE OUT THE CALL OF THE FATHER IN SO MANY AREAS OF OUR EXISTENCE, INCLUDING THE CALL TO GIVE A HOME TO THE ORPHAN. THERE ARE NOT MANY COUPLES WHO HAVE THE AUTHORITY TO GIVE THIS CHARGE TO THE CHURCH, BUT SAMANTHA AND STEVE DO. WE ARE EXCITED THAT IN THIS BOOK THEY HAVE SHARED THEIR STORY AND, MORE IMPORTANTLY, OUR HEAVENLY FATHER'S HEART FOR THE ORPHAN. IT IS OUR PRAYER THAT THE CHURCH WILL HAVE GRACE TO BE A TOOL THROUGH WHICH THE FATHER CAN PLACE EVERY ORPHAN INTO A FAMILY. (PSALM 68:6)"
DAVID AND JEANNETTE MCQUEEN, ADOPTIVE PARENTS
LEAD PASTORS AT BELTWAY PARK CHURCH, ABILENE, TEXAS

"'WALK WITH ME' IS AN INVITATION IN TO THE FATHER HEART OF GOD FOR THE FATHERLESS AND ORPHAN. YOU WILL NOT BE THE SAME PERSON BY THE TIME YOU FINISH READING IT! SAMANTHA'S JOURNEY WITH HER FAMILY DISPLAYS JAMES 1:27 TRUE RELIGION OUT OF RELATIONSHIP WITH GOD.I BELIEVE WITH ALL MY HEART THAT THERE ARE PLACES IN GOD'S HEART THAT WE WILL NEVER GET TO EXPERIENCE IF WE DO NOT SAY "YES" TO HIS HEART FOR ADOPTION, HOWEVER THAT LOOKS FOR EACH ONE OF US."
DANIELLE HELMER
REGIONAL CONFERENCE COORDINATOR, CONTEND GLOBAL

"WALK WITH ME" IS A BOOK THAT REVEALS THE TENDER HEART OF GOD TOWARD ALL OF HIS CHILDREN AND INVITES YOU TO OPEN YOUR'S."
JEFF DOLLAR, SENIOR PASTOR, GRACE CENTER, FRANKLIN, TENNESSEE

ALLEN FAMILY
MINISTRIES

WALK WITH ME
COPYRIGHT © 2019 BY SAMANTHA ALLEN.

SAMANTHA ALLEN
SUPPORT@ALLENFAMILYMINISTRIES.ORG
HTTPS://ALLENFAMILYMINISTRIES.ORG/

$15.95
ISBN 978-1-7338107-0-8

ALLEN FAMILY MINISTRIES BOOKS
ORDER ON AMAZON

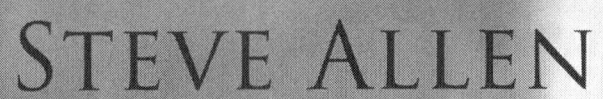

STEVE ALLEN
KINGDOM TREASURES FROM THE LIFE OF ELIJAH AND MY PERSONAL **BATTLE WITH ALS**

AND HE RAN FOR 40 DAYS
A 40 DAY DEVOTIONAL JOURNAL

"FROM A MISSIONARY AND A MENTOR, FROM A FATHER AND A FRIEND, FROM A BUILDER AND A BROTHER, FROM A SAINT WHO HAS SUFFERED, COMES A FORTY DAY FEAST OF A LIFETIME OF WISDOM, THE WORD, AND WONDER."
LOU ENGLE

AND HE RAN FOR 40 DAYS
STEVE ALLEN

"FROM A MISSIONARY AND A MENTOR, FROM A FATHER AND A FRIEND, FROM A BUILDER AND A BROTHER, FROM A SAINT WHO HAS SUFFERED, COMES A FORTY-DAY FEAST OF A LIFETIME OF WISDOM, THE WORD, AND WONDER. FAST FOR FORTY DAYS AND EAT A MEAL A DAY WITH THIS BREAD FROM HEAVEN AND YOU WILL GROW STRONG IN SPIRIT – OR SIMPLY ENJOY THIS DAILY MANNA WHEN YOU WALK WITH GOD IN THE COOL OF THE GARDEN. THEN LIKE STEVE ALLEN, A TRUE ELIJAH FATHER IN THIS GENERATION, YOU'LL HEAR THE STILL SMALL VOICE OF GOD AND RECEIVE A FRESH COMMISSION FROM THE FATHER."

LOU ENGLE
VISIONARY CO-FOUNDER OF THE CALL
AUTHOR OF THE JESUS FAST

AND HE RAN FOR 40 DAYS

In this 40-day devotional journal, Steve Allen shares his story of confronting adversity when he was diagnosed with ALS – Lou Gehrig's disease – in the prime of his life at the age of 48. Given two to five years to live, Steve had to face death head-on and decide what was most important in life.

Steve looks at his own life through the lens of the life of the prophet Elijah, who experienced tremendous spiritual victory on the mountaintop and then was almost crushed by the enemy's threats. Steve applies lessons learned to his own journey living with ALS as he follows Elijah's journey to Mount Sinai where he comes face-to-face with his Creator.

Come participate in your own 40-day journey of self-exploration and learn from these two men what it means to overcome life's adversities and receive your assignment—God's destiny for your life!

Steve loves the mountains and hears the Lord speaking to him through these mighty giants. From trekking with his sons in the Himalayas in Nepal, to looking out from the summit of Pikes Peak, Steve enjoys the outdoors and God's glory manifested through His creation.

Steve is madly in love with Samantha, the woman of his dreams. They have been married for 30 years and have seven children. One, Bethany Hope, is with the Heavenly Father in the House of the Lord. The Allen Family lives in the shadow of the Rockies in Colorado Springs, Colorado, and are engaged in raising up the next generation through discipleship, mentoring, teaching, coaching, and fathering. Steve is on staff with Contend Global Ministries and provides leadership coaching in the business sector.

STEVE & SAMANTHA ALLEN ON TOP OF MASADA IN ISRAEL THE SUMMER OF 2017

ALLEN FAMILY
MINISTRIES

AND HE RAN FOR 40 DAYS
COPYRIGHT © 2019 BY STEVE ALLEN

STEVE ALLEN
SUPPORT@ALLENFAMILYMINISTRIES.ORG
HTTPS://ALLENFAMILYMINISTRIES.ORG

$15.99
ISBN 978-1-7338107-2-2

ALLEN FAMILY MINISTRIES BOOKS
ORDER ON AMAZON

STEVE ALLEN
EXPLORING THE LIFE OF JOSEPH AND THE TRANSFORMATIVE POWER OF A DESTINY FORGED THROUGH SUFFERING

FOREWORD BY LOU ENGLE

JOSEPH
MAN OF SUFFERING
MAN OF DESTINY

JOSEPH MAN OF SUFFERING MAN OF DESTINY
STEVE ALLEN

"READ STEVE'S REFRESHING RETELLING OF JOSEPH'S STORY. DRINK IN HIS WISDOM, DREAM HIS DREAMS, AND FROM YOUR PIT OR YOUR PRISON BE PREPARED FOR A KNOCK ON THE DOOR TO HEAR, "PHARAOH IS CALLING!"

LOU ENGLE
VISIONARY CO-FOUNDER OF THE CALL
AUTHOR OF THE JESUS FAST

JOSEPH, MAN OF SUFFERING, MAN OF DESTINY

After teaching on the life of Joseph for the past 12 years, God dropped a dream in my heart to narrate this incredible story. Come behind the scenes and discover the heart behind the man. On this journey you will meet the men and women who become his friends and some of his worst enemies: Kunré, Omár, Tolik, Myamáll, Nedjém, Neféret, Jabari, Sekhét, Gamál, Nŏur, Sét, and Lotán.

Allow yourself to be transported back almost 3700 years to the time of the pharaohs. Through brilliant pencil sketches, beautiful songs, and inspiring poetry, immerse yourself into the life of Joseph and allow God to speak to you through this amazing son of Jacob. His story is our story. His suffering is our suffering. His destiny is our destiny. Join the journey of a lifetime.

THE VISION JOURNEY

Learn profound lessons from the life of Joseph as we uncover and explore Kingdom treasures from one of the most beloved patriarchs of the Old Testament. Learn why the themes of identity, vision, and destiny are so important for us as believers to understand and implement in our daily lives. From the streets of San Francisco, to the rooftop of the world in the Himalayas, travel with the author, Steve Allen, as he shares nuggets of wisdom that can help transform your life. Learn how to craft a personal vision statement and walk the "Hall of Vision" as you read vision statements and testimonies from men and women of God who have been walking in their callings for decades. Allow their lives to impact yours as you seek to bring glory to the King of Kings!

Steve loves the mountains and hears the Lord speaking to him through these mighty giants. From trekking with his sons in the Himalayas in Nepal, to looking out from the summit of Pikes Peak, Steve enjoys the outdoors and God's glory manifested through His creation.

Steve is madly in love with Samantha, the woman of his dreams. They have been married for 31 years and have seven children. One, Bethany Hope, is with the Heavenly Father in the House of the Lord. The Allen family lives in the shadow of the Rockies in Colorado Springs, Colorado, and raising up the next generation through discipleship, mentoring, teaching, coaching, and fathering. Steve is on staff with Contend Global Ministries and provides leadership coaching in the business sector.

STEVE & SAMANTHA ALLEN ON TOP OF MASADA IN ISRAEL THE SUMMER OF 2017

ALLEN FAMILY MINISTRIES

JOSEPH
MAN OF SUFFERING MAN OF DESTINY
COPYRIGHT © 2020 BY STEVE ALLEN

STEVE ALLEN
SUPPORT@ALLENFAMILYMINISTRIES.ORG
HTTPS://ALLENFAMILYMINISTRIES.ORG

$16.99
ISBN 978-1-7338107-4-6

ALLEN FAMILY MINISTRIES BOOKS
ORDER ON AMAZON

STEVE ALLEN
BECOMING WHAT YOU BEHOLD - A JOURNEY OF TRANSFORMATION BY SEEKING THE HEART OF THE FATHER.
A 31-DAY DEVOTIONAL

10,000 FATHERS

"IF THERE IS A MAN WHO EMBODIES THE FATHER MOVEMENT, IT'S MY FRIEND STEVE ALLEN. SOME WRITE BOOKS. SOME LIVE OUT THEIR BOOKS BEFORE THEY WRITE THEM. EVERY PAGE SPEAKS 'AUTHENTICITY!', AND EVERY WORD IS AN ECHO OF THE APOSTLE PAUL'S 'FOLLOW ME AS I FOLLOW CHRIST.'"
LOU ENGLE

10,000 FATHERS
STEVE ALLEN

"MALACHI PROPHESIED THE COMING OF AN ELIJAH REVOLUTION THAT TURNS THE HEARTS OF FATHERS AND THE CHILDREN TO EACH OTHER IN SUCH POWER THAT IT PREPARES THE WAY FOR THE COMING OF CHRIST. THIS BOOK SURELY MUST BE ONE OF THE SPARKS OF THAT REVOLUTION. IF THERE IS A MAN WHO EMBODIES THAT FATHER MOVEMENT, IT'S MY FRIEND STEVE ALLEN. SOME WRITE BOOKS. SOME LIVE OUT THEIR BOOKS BEFORE THEY WRITE THEM. EVERY PAGE SPEAKS 'AUTHENTICITY!', AND EVERY WORD IS AN ECHO OF THE APOSTLE PAUL'S 'FOLLOW ME AS I FOLLOW CHRIST.' READ, BE CHALLENGED, AND BE SUMMONED INTO THE 10,000 FATHERS REVOLUTION."

LOU ENGLE
VISIONARY CO-FOUNDER OF THE CALL
AUTHOR OF *THE JESUS FAST*

10,000 FATHERS

The attack on fathers and fathering is relentless. For this reason, *10,000 Fathers* was written as a simple but powerful resource to help men grow in their identity as godly fathers, which increases their joy and respect, and gives them renewed purpose as the head of their families. In this 31-day devotional, grow in your character as a man of God and be inspired by the testimonies of godly fathers. This is the hour for men to stand up and lead their wives and children. Join the 10,000 Fathers movement!

In his seventh year battling ALS, Steve has experienced the immutable love of God and the presence of the Holy Spirit that has sustained him through the valley of the shadow of death. Having lost the ability to walk and use his arms, Steve has been strengthened in his faith through over 100 dreams that Father God has sent him through friends and family that have seen his healing. Steve loves the mountains, hearing the Lord speaking to him through these mighty giants. From trekking with his sons in the Himalayas, to looking out from the summit of Pikes Peak, Steve enjoys the outdoors and God's glory manifested through His creation. Steve is madly in love with Samantha, the woman of his dreams; they have been married for 32 years and have seven children. One, Bethany Hope, is with the Heavenly Father in the House of the Lord. The Allen family lives in the shadow of the Rockies in Colorado Springs, Colorado, and is raising up the next generation through discipleship, mentoring, teaching, coaching, and fathering. Steve is on staff with Contend Global Ministries and is the founder of Allen Leadership Coaching.

STEVE & SAMANTHA ALLEN ON TOP OF MASADA IN ISRAEL THE SUMMER OF 2017

ALLEN FAMILY MINISTRIES

10,000 FATHERS
COPYRIGHT © 2021 BY STEVE ALLEN

STEVE ALLEN
STEVE@ALLENCOACHING.COM
WWW.ALLENCOACHING.COM

$17.95
ISBN 978-1-7338107-6-0

COMING IN 2023

STEVE ALLEN

ENTRUSTED

RAISING WORLD CHANGERS AND HISTORY MAKERS AT THE END OF THE AGE

ENTRUSTED
Raising World Changers and History Makers at the End of the Age

Scott held his breath as he sped through the red light. Several cars slammed on their brakes, honking furiously as they narrowly missed hitting him.

I need to stop doing this, Scott thought to himself. I'm tired of being late for my family.

The wheels squealed on his Audi as he took a hard right turn onto Howell Street, only four blocks from Jonathan's soccer field. He racked his brain: When was his game supposed to start? Was it 5 or 6? A tinge of guilt crept into Scott's conscience as he realized that he had missed three soccer games and a music recital in the last month.

If only Jessica would get off my back. Doesn't she know, I'm doing this for the family? He found himself distracted by the sports cars in the parking lot. Wow! He thought. A Porsche 911 would look great in my driveway. He realized he was already spending the bonus even before it was official.

If Scott knew the storm brewing on the horizon, he would have known money was not going to save him.

*****

The above excerpt from Entrusted is a reflection of many families in today's American culture.

Entrusted is divided into two parts. Part one is a modern-day fable that illustrates the challenges that many families face today. Part two unpacks biblical kingdom principles that will equip fathers and mothers to intentionally raise sons and daughters who know their identity, walk in their purpose, and live with spiritual vision.

The end-times clock is ticking, and time is running out. The King is returning. Will we be prepared and – more importantly – will our children?

ALLENCOACHING
v i s i o n . e m p o w e r e d

Leadership Coach

SPECIAL OFFER FROM
ALLEN LEADERSHIP COACHING

FREE 30-MINUTE VISION COACHING CALL

CONTACT:
steve@allencoaching.com
ALLENCOACHING.COM

Made in the USA
Columbia, SC
29 October 2022